Donkey Baseball and Other Sporting Delights

ALSO BY GILES TIPPETTE

Donkey Baseball

& Other Sporting Delights

by Giles Tippette

Taylor Publishing Company
Dallas, Texas

Design by David Timmons

Published by Taylor Publishing Company
                1550 West Mockingbird Lane
                Dallas, Texas 75235

Some of the chapters in this book originally appeared
in *Sports Illustrated* and *Texas Monthly*.

Library of Congress Cataloging-in-Publication Data
Tippette, Giles.
Donkey baseball and other sporting delights / Giles Tippette.
    p.   cm.
    ISBN 0-87833-668-0 : $15.95
    1. Sports—Anecdotes. I. Title
GV707.T54 1989
796'.0207—dc20   89-30433 CIP

Printed in the United States of America

10 9 8 7 6 5 4 3 2 1

To Betsyanne, my wife,
a Yankee who thinks girls' field hockey
is a major sport

Contents

Foreword

There is an anecdote that defines Giles Tippette about as well as anyone can. This was nearly twenty years ago, the week of an annual bacchanal known as the Livestock Show and Rodeo, and Giles had stopped for a refreshment in the bar of a Houston hotel.

He was dressed in the proper vestments—the hat, the boots, the belt buckle. He had been tagging along with a world-class cowboy, Larry Mahan, researching a book that became *The Brave Men*.

A stranger two barstools over sized him up. "You in the rodeo?" asked the stranger.

"I'm a writer," replied Tippette, not snobby, mind you, just matter-of-fact.

"What do you ride?"

"I ride a typewriter."

No telling how far this conversation could have gone, except that the stranger soon realized that they were not quite receiving each other.

When it became clear that Giles was a w-r-i-t-e-r, not a r-i-d-e-r, the stranger introduced himself. He was Bill Peterson, recently of Florida State, then the new Rice football coach. And out of that encounter came another book, a season with the Rice football team, called *Saturday's Children*.

I always had the impression that Giles, one way or another, stumbled into more good stories than most writers do on purpose. But an additional point begs to be made: he and Bill Peterson were both right. Tippette is a writer and a rider—planes, trains, cars, boats and bulls, hard landings and soft, a tale in every blessed one.

But sportswriting was not, is not, the craft of Giles Tippette. His craft is writing, about people, and some of those people happen to play at sport. Giles is among the best at finding the blood, sweat, fear, and fun in all of it. I've always enjoyed Giles's work for the sheer pleasure of reading the words, and that sentiment has nothing to do with his having paid me the highest compliment of my life. This was a few months before we had actually met. I heard his name—a wonderful name, I wish I had thought of it—for the first time from a beautiful receptionist at the William Morris agency in New York. Giles had been there on a day I happened to call. She was impressed, and a little stunned, by him. He was tall, rangy, ruggedly good-looking, twangy voiced, super confident. He did not look like a writer, she said, but he surely fit her idea of a real Texan.

When she asked if we knew each other, Giles told her a story. He was in college, married, struggling, and unable to afford subscriptions to the two newspapers that were delivered daily. He kept *The Houston Post*, he told her, so he could read my stories in the sports section.

Well, hell, we were destined to be friends for life.

Allow what you will for personal bias. I read several of the pieces included in this anthology when they first appeared. I found in the re-reading that time had taken away none of their richness. In the introduction to a piece on rodeoing, Giles observes, "Sometimes I think that the worst thing about making friends is the risk of losing them."

Turn to any page. There is a phrase, a piece of dialogue, an original way with words that will pull you into the text. He makes it seem easy. No writer worth his salt will admit, of course, that the work is ever easy. If reading Giles Tippette makes it seem so, the answer is in the attitude. He treats words as one would a good friend.

—MICKEY HERSKOWITZ

Introduction

A t one point in my life I thought I wanted to get rich; at another I thought I wanted to be sane. But it seemed like sports kept getting in the way of both goals. Sort of.

I can't say they got completely in the way of the first because they certainly afforded me the opportunity, an opportunity I wouldn't ordinarily have had, to receive a college education. Which is, I guess, fundamental in getting rich. If you use it.

I can't speak for the second because there is too much evidence to the contrary. No sane man does what I did in some of the stories you'll read in this anthology, certainly no sane man of advancing age.

But I did 'em.

And I did 'em because I've always felt at home with sports. Now that may seem like a peculiar expression—to feel at home with sports. But I always felt more at home in the locker room or in the arena than I did at my mother's table.

Of course you didn't eat at my mother's table and I reckon that's where it started. At fifteen I was a junior at Bay City (Texas) High School with a burning desire to be a jock. Except I was already 6'2" tall and a solid 130 pounds.

Not exactly your premium build for an athlete.

Now while my contemporaries in school were being fed meat and potatoes and gravy, my mother, who had read some book called *You Are What You Eat*, was feeding me and my stepfather on glass-top tables and napkin rings and salads. Obviously I wasn't gaining much weight on that diet and neither was my stepfather,

Don Jackson. Came a day and I got home from school and discovered some few pounds of ground beef in the refrigerator. Jackson was home early from work and I announced I was going to make a meat loaf. Now I had no more idea of how to make a meat loaf than a jackass knows how to run in the Kentucky Derby, but I was determined that it was try or starve.

Jackson said, "You better leave that meat alone. I reckon your mother is going to make some kind of salad out of it."

I think I said something to the effect of the hell with it, I can't be punished anymore.

So I jumbled that meat together, threw in a couple of raw eggs, crumbled up some crackers, and added it to the mixture and pronounced it finished. Except Jackson, who always had an inquisitive streak in him, came in and asked if, since I was going for nutrition, I hadn't ought to put some carbohydrates in it. Consequently we mixed in some mashed potatoes, poured on about half a bottle of catsup for piquancy, and threw it in the oven.

When my mother got home, Jackson and I were sitting at that glass-top dining table eating three-inch-thick slices of meat loaf. My mother took one horrified look and said, "What are you two doing!"

Jackson just looked up at her mildly and said, "Well, we're eating for a change."

That summer I worked for Dahnes Drugstore in Bay City delivering prescriptions. My day started by going by Smith's Grocery and drinking two quarts of milk. At lunch I went down to the Walgreen's drugstore and ate two hamburgers with an egg malt. Then when I got off at six o'clock I'd go over to Etie's cafe and eat a double order of chicken-fried steak. After that I went home and ate the salad my mother had prepared for my supper. I'd been ousted from the kitchen by my mother, but I didn't suffer. Jackson may have, but I gained sixty pounds that summer and went on from there. By the time my senior year started I was 6'3" and weighed in at a little over 190 pounds. In my senior year I set an interscholastic record for the 180-yard low hurdles, got a tryout with the St. Louis Cardinals baseball team, and was given a football scholarship to John Tarleton Junior College.

I also started getting dates with actual girls, girls who before couldn't see me for the green paint in the school hallways. I know that today the jock has to compete with those accomplished musicians and poets who know three chords on a guitar and where the EXTRA LOUD button is on their amplifiers, but in my day that wasn't the case.

So I don't know what hooked me. Maybe it was the girls, maybe it was the feeling of being down on the playing field with the crowd yelling, maybe it was the camaraderie that athletics produces.

Maybe it was all of those and several elements not mentioned. All I know is that I got hooked.

And it wasn't just track and football and baseball, it was rodeo and any other kind of sport that represented a challenge to what my better judgment told me not to get involved in.

Except basketball. I never liked basketball. Partly, I think, because I couldn't play it and partly because I once lost out to a basketball player over a mighty pretty girl.

As near as I can tell, rodeo was the dumbest activity I ever engaged in. I rode all three bucking events, primarily bulls, and your grandmother would have been better. I mean I'd have had to work my way up to mediocre.

But I persisted. To the detriment of my aching body and quite a number of broken bones.

I think the older I got the more I enjoyed participating. I don't think I appreciated the little talent I had when I was young. It wasn't much—mainly built around speed. I couldn't pick up the spin on a curve ball and I wasn't what you'd call a hard hitter in football, but I always managed to get by with that speed that you just get as a gift. And, of course, when you're young you just take gifts for granted.

So I think it was as I aged and, on a few occasions was able to pry a performance out of my reluctant body that I began to appreciate, truly, just what being an athlete meant. It wasn't just the roar of the crowd; it wasn't walking back up the track after you'd set a record, or even stealing second and third base consecutively. It was a lot more than that. It was the smell of liniment in the trainer's room, the crisp feel of the air around your body when you knew you'd put it in as good a shape as you could; the kidding, the digging that athletes do to each other.

It's a very special world and one that comes and goes so quickly that very often you don't have time to appreciate it except in retrospect.

I don't know at what point I phased out of being a jock and

became a sportswriter. I'm not sure it's happened yet. I think it may have occurred about 1971. I'd published a book about big-time college football called *Saturday's Children* that had been serialized in *Sports Illustrated.* At about that time, near the age of thirty-five, I must have been going through male menopause because I'd decided to go back and try my hand one more time at rodeoing. I'd gotten myself entered in a little jackpot rodeo in Fulshear, Texas, in the bull riding. By then, I'd published a few books and written a number of magazine articles and there had been some publicity in the Houston papers about me as a writer.

All of which was fine and dandy and I was grateful. Except that when I started to get down on this old bull at Fulshear the rodeo announcer started saying, "And now, ladies and gentlemen, we have a special treat for you. Coming out of chute number four is a well-known writer who's written for *Time, Newsweek,* and *Sports Illustrated.* In addition he's written—"

Except the bull wasn't paying any attention. He was cutting up in the chute and slinging those strings of slobber back at me and turning his head and looking at me with a malevolent eye and promising me what he was going to do when he got me out in the arena. I remember listening to that announcer's words and thinking, wildly, "Hell, don't tell the crowd! Tell the bull! The bull ain't impressed."

In my day I've known some of the better recognized names in sports. A little bit as a player, but mostly as a sportswriter. As a general rule they're mostly pretty good folks, but I've known a few that would tear your head off and then politely inquire if you had any hats you wouldn't be needing.

None of them impressed me any more than the guys I played with back in high school. Because it's still athletics, no matter what level. And I'm not planning on getting impressed until the bull does and I think he's still got a fixed opinion on that.

So I don't know if I ever really made the change from athlete to sportswriter. I've known a lot of sportswriters who hung around and hung on every word these giants emoted. I didn't. As far as I was concerned we were still all out there in the arena together.

And I have the fixed opinion that I never really made the transition, never really hung them up. I recall one of my editors at *Sports Illustrated,* Linda Verigan, saying to me, "Giles, it's not necessary you get yourself killed for this story. Remember, it's just a story and just a game."

Except I never felt that way. I always wanted to take my readers right into the action and I never believed that sports was just a game. I always thought of it as a way of life.

So all I've tried to do with the following stories is introduce you to a side of sports you might not have seen. All I hope is that, in reading them, you have the same amount of fun that I did in participating.

But take them for what they were; a hell of a lot of fun. Sometimes I get a little full of myself and start telling my wife stories that get bigger and faster every year. She has a way of bringing me up short. She says, "Now, if I understand correctly, this was a career that started with a meat loaf?"

Never, never, tell your wife about matters that can be used against you in the last word.

1

Vaulting for the Sky

Of all the stories in this collection I suppose this one, in retrospect, frightens me more than all the others put together. A lot of years have passed since this story happened and, during that time, I became a high-time pilot with a commercial license and advanced ratings. For a relatively brief period I even made somewhat of a living flying different people on somewhat less than orthodox errands. And during all those thousands of flying hours, flying over clutching mountains and through disapproving weather, I don't think I ever had more reason to be frightened than I should have been about the events that occurred in this story.

I say should have been because, at the time it happened, I didn't have sense enough to be scared. It's only now, looking back, that I shudder and remind my children of just how close they came to never being.

I also had one other quite unexpected problem with the story. Sports Illustrated *has a staff of researchers obviously trained by the Internal Revenue Service. Their job is to come right along behind you and check every fact, every name, every date, every anything that's in the story. I think they pretty well live for the opportunity to catch a writer in a mistake, be it willful or careless. So, because of that, I've always been very careful to get all my ducks in a row before I set out on a story.*

And, since my mother was in this one, I thought I'd better call to make sure she remembered it exactly as I did.

She not only didn't remember it as I did, she didn't remember it at all. In fact she said it hadn't happened.

Well, that was sort of a shock, especially since I'd been there my ownself and had memories of it to the point of nightmares. I sat around frustrated for a time and then I took my mother's psyche into account. My mother isn't afraid of flying; she'd just prefer to think it doesn't exist. She was blocking.

So, with no little effort, I was finally able to run down that first flight instructor of mine, Elmo Hatcher. Elmo is eighty-four, but he remembered it as if it were yesterday. When I called my mother to tell her what Elmo had said, she replied, a little frigidly, "A man his age, drinking! He ought to be ashamed."

So come relive with me the frightening skies of a ten-year-old.

I soloed an airplane when I was about ten years old. It's hard to say exactly how old I was because I wasn't as conscious of age and time then as I am now. I'll admit, though, that on that particular day—it was probably in 1944 or '45—I came close to discovering something most kids don't know: We're all mortal.

My soloing took place over Bay City, Texas, where I did most of my growing up. A man there named Elmo Hatcher was a friend of my mother and stepfather. Elmo was a pilot, the kind of fellow boys my age just naturally gravitated toward.

His airplane was a fairly ancient Aeronca, a two-seat, low-wing craft capable of cruising about 70 mph with a good tail wind. But it was an airplane, and it represented part of my dream for the future. I hadn't quite decided if I wanted to be a professional ballplayer and a pilot, or to pursue my probable destiny as the first man to pole-vault fifteen feet. In that era most people considered that height impossible, but I had always known I was bound for high places. So, day after day, there I was in my backyard, armed with a stout cane pole. I had already attained the dizzying height of 6'6" and considered the next eight and a half feet a mere formality.

My future as an aviator got a boost from all the time I spent at the airport hanging around Elmo and his airplane. Despite my mother's strong disapproval, he had let me fly with him many times. I started out in the right (copilot's) seat, but when I was tall enough to reach the rudder pedals, Elmo would sometimes let me fly in the left seat and practice takeoffs and landings. At first he guided me through, letting me follow him on the controls, but after a time he began to lounge back in his seat and keep his hands and feet to himself while I flew the plane.

One Sunday, late in the summer, my parents went out to the

airport with me, even though planes made my mother nervous. Well, that day Elmo and I took a short hop, and after we landed, we taxied over to the hangars where my parents were standing.

Elmo opened his door, got out and said, "You about ready to take it on your own? Solo?"

"Sure," I said, with a nonchalance born of ignorance.

"Go ahead then," he said, shutting the door. "Take it around the patch and land."

I didn't think any more about it. The fact that I had never been alone in an airplane before didn't enter my mind. I just lined up on the runway, poured on the power, reached flying speed and took off. I made the standard climbing left turn, put the plane on the downwind leg, reached pattern altitude and leveled off. I don't remember being particularly nervous at that point. The presence of my instructor lingered, and I was automatically doing the things I had been taught. Then I made a left turn that would take me to the final approach.

At the proper moment I reached out and pulled out the throttle—or what I thought was the throttle; actually it was the knob to control the carburetor heat, which had nothing to do with increasing or decreasing power—and tilted the nose down to set up my glide path for the landing. Now, you don't land a light plane with the power on; you pull the throttle back to idle and control your speed with the angle of attack. As I guided the airplane toward the ground, lining up on the runway, I became aware of a strange feeling. I realized it was going much faster than it was supposed to, and there was that roaring sound that a powerplant makes at full throttle. I glanced at the airspeed indicator and saw I was doing 90 mph. Even as I watched, it started creeping toward the red line at a hundred.

I had descended to three hundred and was well on my way to a high-speed crash. It was also about then that I became excruciatingly aware that I was in that plane all by myself. Total fear took over. I could think only that the throttle must be stuck, so I pushed and pulled the carburetor heat knob several times, but to no avail. The knob I wanted, the throttle, was right beside the carburetor heat control. The carburetor knob was yellow, and the throttle was white. I had manipulated that white knob a hundred times, but now—in one of those odd lapses that can befuddle the human mind at any age—it never entered my mind that it had anything to do with the throttle. I had fixed on that yellow knob, convinced it controlled the power.

I didn't crash. At two hundred feet some instinct caused me to pull back on the wheel, climb, and make a go-around. Once again I flew the pattern, set up on my final approach, and pulled the carburetor heat knob. And once again I had to make a go-around.

Meanwhile, on the ground, I've been told, my mother asked Elmo who was in the airplane with me. He said, "Well, Grace, there were just the two of us in it before, and I got out. I guess that just leaves him."

That's when she began screaming at Elmo, "Get him down!"

Elmo replied, "Well, Grace, that ain't a kite up there. I can't just reel him in like he was on a string. Don't worry, he'll be all right." I'm sure Elmo meant it. Of course, that was before my second go-around. After that, I doubt he could have said anything that would have done much to reassure my mother. Her nervousness had turned to hysteria.

Naturally, I didn't know any of this. I was busy flying around and around the airstrip, vainly pushing in and pulling out the yellow knob. By now Elmo had figured out what my problem was. There was no radio in the Aeronca, so he had to go up and get me.

He borrowed a Piper Cub from another pilot, and the next thing I knew he was flying alongside me holding a message in large black letters on his window: PULL OUT WHITE KNOB. Naturally I did it. Automatically. Despite the fact that I had not even begun my approach. I pulled out the throttle and the roar from the engine became a gentle, idling purr. The airplane started to descend. Again, for some odd reason, my mind went blank. Instead of merely pushing the throttle in and picking up more speed, I nursed the airplane as far downwind as I could, maintaining a speed just above stalling, then made two gentle left turns and landed. I brought the plane to a stop, wheeled it around and stared at the two knobs, still wondering which one I should push to get up taxi power.

I thought that was the end of the episode (except for the state my mother stayed in for about a week), but some ten years later I was accepted into the Aviation Cadet Program of the U.S. Air Force. While at preflight training, I wrote my mother and said Elmo Hatcher was my instructor. It had to be taken as a joke. Everyone knew that they don't let cadets in preflight near airplanes. But I hadn't taken into account my mother's continuing lack of knowledge about aviation.

Two weeks later I was summoned by my commanding officer. I went with fear and trembling. He had a letter in his hand, and he wanted to know who or what an Elmo Hatcher was. It seemed that my mother had written her congressman a colorful letter insisting she wouldn't have her son instructed in the air by "highly unorthodox persons." That congressman had passed on the letter to the Air Force, and it had finally filtered down to my CO. I stammered out an explanation, but the officer was not amused. I spent the next two weekends marching punishment tours —six hours a day for four days.

You march punishment tours in white gloves. During those hours I had a lot of time to study my gloves and memorize the color white. It's not the same color as yellow. Yellow is the color of the carburetor heat knob. White is the throttle knob. White is the color that makes airplanes go up and down.

By the way, though I became a pilot, I never did play professional baseball. And I didn't become the first man to clear fifteen feet in the pole vault. But I'm dead-solid perfect on white now.

2

Uncle Joe and the Headless Horseman

Of all the men I've known I guess I'd say that Uncle Slick was the greatest influence. He wasn't the smartest of men in a scholastic sense, in fact I don't think he even graduated from high school. But I reckon I learned more from him, subliminally, than from anyone I've ever known. He had a wit that he could jab you with that was every bit as lethal as that stubby forefinger he carried around like a cattle prod. And when he said something you generally remembered it.

In the twenty-odd years I fished with him I don't recall any two trips being the same.

With one exception. . . I always seemed to find a way to foul up. And to foul up in a way that left me as wide open as possible to Uncle Slick's jabs. I sometimes used to think he only took me along for comic relief.

And it didn't matter how I'd done athletically, or, later, how many books I'd published or what magazine article I'd written, I was still "Junior" and would always remain so. He once told me that it was a constant source of wonder to him how I could always be the only one in the boat that wasn't catching fish. He'd say, sadly, "Junior, you've got to quit fishing up in the trees and out on the bank. The fish are in the water, son, and that's where you ought to fish."

One day, some years back, he met up with a very unfair heart attack. I shall continue to miss him.

believe it was the knife sheath that caused my Uncle Joe Jackson to refer to me as the Headless Horseman for a good deal more years than I'd care to remember. The horseman part came because I was a rodeo cowboy; the headless part was because of something I'd done one day while we were fishing. We were in a little boat about ten feet off the shore of Day Lake, which is a tributary of the Trinity River in East Texas, close to Dayton. This was back in 1951, when I was a levelheaded sixteen-year-old who might have known an apple from an orange if you'd peeled them first.

I'd recently acquired a first-class filleting and general fish knife that cost about $15, which considerably damaged my dating and general running around fund. Naturally, I was proud of that knife and didn't intend to loan it to any careless persons with poor character references.

I'd saved up my money and bought that knife because my Uncle Joe had told me that any man who could stand upright in a fishing boat ought to have one. Now my Uncle Joe (whom I sometimes called Uncle Slick because of his bald head) was the best fisherman I'd ever known. I knew this was true because he'd told me so on several occasions.

On this particular day we were tied to the limb of a fallen cypress tree and were bobber fishing for perch or crappie or any other fish dumb enough to wander into our reach. We used minnows for bait. I realize there are sport fishermen out there who would cringe at the prospect of bobber fishing with minnows, considering such a practice as sport only for children using bent pins at the end of twine on a cane pole. They wouldn't have held that opinion long in the presence of my Uncle Joe. He was an iconoclast of the first water, a man whose main quarry was the "wily soccali," which was what he liked to call the black crappie or the perch. He didn't even like bass and would seldom boat them. As a matter of fact he often referred to bait casters as "evildoers who thrash the water to a froth and threaten to ruin the fishing for honest men."

I once went fishing with him in the company of the outdoors columnist for the *Houston Chronicle*. Uncle Joe and I were bobber fishing; the columnist was making long casts to the opposite bank in search of bass. He'd caught, maybe, a couple, the best going no more than four pounds. At some point I got lucky and snagged a lunker bass that may have weighed eight pounds. The columnist was at the front of the boat, I was at the rear and Uncle Joe was in the middle. I'd removed the hook from the bass and was sitting there grinning and holding it up for all to admire, when Uncle Joe reached over, took the fish by the gills and threw it back into the lake. "Get that eely monster out of the boat!" he said. The columnist never did speak directly to Uncle Joe again.

Despite his peculiar preferences, my uncle wasn't as casual a fisherman as you might think from his use of bobbers and minnows. On other occasions he was as dedicated in his pursuit of trout as any fisherman ever outfitted by Abercrombie & Fitch. His "cane" pole was the finest split-bamboo fly rod you could buy, and his line was a tapered, weighted beauty that told him exactly what was going on beneath the surface of the water. Even in bobber fishing, while the rest of us in the boat would cuss the goggle-eye perch that kept nipping off our bait, Uncle Joe would pop them into the boat for cut bait. He used to tell me, "Junior [which was a name I thought I hated until I became the Headless Horseman], you got to be smarter than the fish."

But back to our outing on Day Lake. I had snagged a pretty good perch and had boated it. The problem was that the hook was deep in its throat, and I couldn't get it out. So I finally took out my brand-new filleting knife and set out to cut the hook loose. It was going well until the fish gave a sudden flop, and its dorsal fin stuck me in the hand. With that, the fish and my knife went overboard.

Well, I was stunned. I was just flat stunned. I sat there for a few seconds and then in a fit of rage I hurled the sheath after the knife. Uncle Joe was in the front of the boat, and he turned around and looked at me. He didn't say anything for a moment. As I've mentioned, Day Lake was a tributary of the Trinity River—sometimes. By that I mean that, on occasion, the Trinity backed up into the lake, producing a current. This was such an occasion.

Uncle Joe said, "Junior, have you considered that your knife went overboard in about three feet of water and, since we've got the exact spot marked, you could probably find it by wading around for a few minutes?"

I slapped my forehead. I said, "Oh, hell yes, why didn't I think of that!"

He looked over behind him. "But you've thrown your sheath in the water, and it's now floating downstream."

I looked where he was looking. The sheath had reached midstream and was bobbing along in the brown water, now about fifteen yards away. I said, "I can fix that!"

I was only wearing jeans, it being summer, so I just upped on the side of the boat and dove in. I caught up with the sheath about fifty yards downstream. Meanwhile, Uncle Joe had untied the rope from the tree limb and had paddled his way down to get me. After a little maneuvering I was back in the boat. I had the sheath and held it up, water streaming off me. I said, "Well, now, what do you think of that? Got it back, didn't I?"

He didn't say anything for a long minute. Then he just pointed back from whence we'd come. I looked. All along that bank were fallen cypress trees that looked exactly like the one we'd been tied up next to. My knife was now buried in the mud below the brown water at an unknown site. I had recovered the sheath, but had lost the knife. That's like being married without a wife. I thought for a minute that it was Uncle Joe, not me, who had lost sight of the spot where my knife went in. If he hadn't untied the boat and come downstream to pick me up, I'd have got them both back.

But Uncle Joe just grinned at me as he grabbed hold of the oars. He said, "Junior, have I ever recounted to you a tale by Washington Irving?"

Uncle Joe wasn't an educated man in formal terms, but he knew as much about literature, the kind he wanted to know, as any man I've ever met. And he could tell it. He could even stop a poker game—a *poker* game, mind you—with his recitation of Robert Service's poem *The Shooting of Dan McGrew*. So I knew I was in for it.

Still looking at me and still rowing, he laughed malevolently, "Heh, heh, heh." Now my Uncle Joe was a compact man with Popeye-like forearms and strong, square hands. He had a habit, which wasn't going to win him any votes, of jabbing you in the chest with his right forefinger when he was trying to make a point. It was like being hit with a small pile driver. It wouldn't actually separate your ribs from your sternum, but it could, depending on the duration of the point he was insisting you agree with him on, make laughing a painful matter for some days afterward.

I had, on many occasions, been the recipient of that forefinger, but, as much as I hated it, I hated that "heh, heh, heh" much worse. It meant he had you by the nape of the neck and, struggle as you might, you weren't going to get loose.

So he said, "Well, Junior, this is *The Legend of Sleepy Hollow.* Or the tale of the Headless Horseman." Then he commenced to tell me the story, dwelling with some relish on just how dumb Ichabod Crane was and how he was made to lose sight of his objective by the Headless Horseman who assailed him in a moonlit lane. He even went into some detail on the possibility of my resemblance to Ichabod Crane (as well he might, for I was rather tall and slim at that time).

Then he paused and looked thoughtful, resting on the oars. He said, "But then I don't reckon you were any dumber than the Headless Horseman. Hell, all he had was a pumpkin for a head."

It could have been worse.

He could have called me Ichabod.

3

Hotfooting to Victory

This story actually embarrasses me. When you read it you'll no doubt realize why. In fact, even though I'd set a fairly good track record in it, I was reluctant, for many years, to set it down on paper.

It's hard to imagine anyone, even a scatterbrained teenager, doing something quite so stupid and then aggravating it by continued stupidity. You'll meet Rooster Andrews in this story and, many years later, when I saw him in his sporting-goods store in Austin the first thing he said to me was, "Can you explain to me how come you did what you did?" He said, "I mean, I've thought about that off and on through the years and, Giles, it just didn't make any sense."

And it doesn't make any sense. The initial mistake was bad enough. But to go ahead and compound it as I did—wow!

The only reason I exposed myself to this chagrin was that one night I told my wife the story and she said I ought to write it up for Sports Illustrated. *Well, I'd been wanting to go to the Bahamas and my wife had said we couldn't afford it. I'd said what if I do the story and get a check from* Sports Illustrated? *Can we go then?*

She'd said yes and I'd done the story and got paid. But I still lost.

They have a gambling casino in Nassau. This whole episode was a mistake from beginning to end. Thirty years later I still got burned on this Pyrrhic victory.

'm going to tell you a story about an incident that only two other people know about. One of them has forgotten it; the other one was sworn to secrecy. It's about how I came to set the record for the Black Cat Relays in the 180-yard low hurdles.

I have kept silent all these years because the story makes me look like a damn fool. The only reason I'm willing to speak out now is in the hope it might help young athletes understand that mistakes, however foolish, must be dealt with at the time of their inception.

The story begins with a thunderstorm the evening before the Black Cat Relays. This was back in April 1952, in Bay City, Texas, and the Black Cat Relays was one of the premier track meets in that part of the country. I was pretty excited that night, and not without reason. I wasn't much in the high hurdles, but the longer low-hurdles event seemed to fit my stride and my tall, skinny frame. My times had been improving, and it was not totally out of line to think I might have a chance against the athletes from some of the bigger schools in Houston and Galveston. Besides all that, I was particularly interested in impressing a girl who was going to be in the stands. (She later married a rice farmer who couldn't have beaten your Aunt Martha in a flight of hurdles.)

After supper the night before the meet, I was trying to relax with the radio when the most violent thunderstorm I had ever heard burst in the skies over Bay City. The thunder boomed and rumbled, the wind blew, and hail hit the roof and windows as though it had been shot from a cannon. In between the thunderclaps, the lightning flashed so brightly that it looked to be about noon outside. The static on the radio was so bad you couldn't tell if it was Eddie Fisher or Patti Page singing. Finally, around eight o'clock, the storm turned into the homestretch, gave one final kick and blew out every bit of electricity on our side of town.

Time to get out the candles. Normally I would put this disruption to good use: scaring the hell out of my little brother with ghost stories, waiting for the ice cream in the freezer section of the refrigerator to get in such desperate straits that it would have to be eaten immediately, reading by candlelight and pretending to be Abraham Lincoln.

But this night was not the same. I was too nervous and excited about the track meet to enjoy it. I needed peace and quiet to compose myself and prepare my body and mind for a third-place finish. I had no thought of winning, not against the kind of competition I knew to expect. Third place would be a major victory for me.

We sat around until ten o'clock, waiting for the lights to come back on. I was getting more nervous by the minute. Finally my family went to bed, and after sitting there for a while, I decided that I ought to at least rest my legs by lying down, even though I knew I couldn't sleep. I got a candle and lit my way into my bedroom and undressed. I set the candle down beside my bed and crawled between the sheets, listening to the last of the storm groaning and grumbling as it moved on. I wasn't worried about the meet being rained out. Such spring storms were common in our part of the country. They would come in, raise hell for a couple of hours and then go on away, never to be heard from again.

I lay there for a while, stiff as a board except for an occasional nervous twitch. I tell you, without being able to read or listen to the radio or distract my mind in any other way from the track meet, it was terribly hard to compose myself. I was so desperate for distraction that I would probably have played Go Fish or Old Maid with my little brother if he had been awake. Finally, I decided it would be a good idea to go to the kitchen and check on the condition of the quart of strawberry ice cream I knew would be in critical danger. So I threw the sheet back and swung my legs over the side of the bed. I set my feet down. My right foot hit the floor. My left foot landed directly on top of the candle that was guttering in a saucer full of molten wax.

It got my attention. It got my attention like nothing had ever done before. I don't think I actually reached the ceiling on my first spring, but I think I got it on subsequent leaps as I went jumping and hopping around my bedroom. I don't know for sure, because when I put the candle out with my foot, the room had gone pitch-black, and I may have just been hitting the walls of the room rather than the ceiling.

I didn't yell—not out of consideration for the rest of the family but simply because I didn't have the breath. Just set your foot down on a lighted candle sometime and see how much breath you have.

After a time, I figured that rolling around on the floor with my teeth gritted wasn't helping, so I stepped and hopped my way to the bathroom. I turned on the cold water in the tub and put my foot under it. The relief was instant, but with the absence of pain came the sudden realization that I might have done myself considerable injury and that one-legged hurdlers don't even finish third.

My stepfather came into the bathroom holding a candle. I figured he must have been awakened by the sound of the water. He said, "What in the hell have you been doing, gymnastics? I never heard such a racket in my life." By that time he was close enough to hold the candle down and see my foot. I was afraid, but I looked too. Naturally it was the ball of my foot I had set on the candle. I could already see a blister forming under the layer of wax. It was the size of a quarter and growing. My stepfather asked me what I had done. I told him.

"Well," he said, "you have exceeded yourself. I thought last week when you nearly killed the cat with the lawn-mower that you had reached your potential, but I see you have uncounted reserves left."

I didn't know what he meant and I didn't care. I got out something about the track meet. He said, "Oh, I wouldn't worry. You being on the team, you ought to be able to get a good seat in the stands."

I told him I had to compete, that my life and future depended on it. I told him that if I didn't compete and the reason why I didn't ever got out, I would be ruined for life and would probably never be able to get another date until I was thirty years old and living in some other state.

Well, maybe I didn't really say that, but it was close enough to give him the picture of how serious I considered the matter. He said, "Well, we got maybe one chance. We got to draw that blister and toughen it up, and the only thing I know that will do that is salt water. But it's going to hurt."

I said I didn't care, that I could stand a pain in my foot but not in my heart. He just gave me an odd look and said he hoped I didn't go around town talking like that. He also said, "And if I was you I would be sure and not wake up your mother. If she gets a look at that foot you won't be going out of this house, much less to a track meet."

While I limped back into the bedroom, my stepfather went into the kitchen and put a little water in a pan, got out the salt and the bottle of iodine. He put a lot of salt in the water and about half the bottle of iodine. I wanted to know what the iodine was for, and he said infection. I couldn't see the point to that, since I associated iodine with cuts and I didn't have a cut. Then he got a razor blade and slit the blister, and I understood. I understood even better when he stuck my foot into the salt-iodine-water solution. I understook so well that I nearly bit my lower lip off trying not to scream and wake up my mother.

It took about fifteen minutes before I could keep my foot in the pan without my stepfather holding it there, but he was finally able to let go. He stood up, shook his head and said, "Now about all you can do is sit there, as long as you can stay awake, and soak your foot. It might work."

Indeed, it did seem to work. The next morning I bandaged my foot and put on thick socks and tennis shoes. I had a slight limp, but it was less from pain than from not wanting to put any weight on the ball of my foot. At breakfast my stepfather asked me how my blister was doing, and I said, "Well, at least we know there's no danger of infection." I said it sarcastically, because I was pretty sure he had put a good deal more iodine in the water than was necessary.

My main concern was hiding my latest misadventure from my track coach, Joe Rogers. He already had enough ammunition against me to seriously question whether I had the mental and physical aptitude for track.

The preliminaries for the low hurdles were at ten that morning. I was in the second heat. I got dressed without anyone noticing anything, but during my warmups, through the thin sole of my track shoe, I could already feel a tenderness starting that was shortly going to bring tears to my eyes. I was warming up on the infield grass rather than on the cinder track when Coach Rogers noticed me. He came over and said, "What's the matter with you? Get over there on the track. You don't see any hurdles set up out here, do you?"

Now, it was Coach Rogers's habit to give all his sprinters and hurdlers a Hershey bar about thirty minutes before their event, obviously on the assumption that the sugar would give them that explosive energy necessary for a good start out of the blocks. I had eaten my Hershey bar, but all it did was make me feel a little sick to my stomach. Or something made me feel sick to my stomach.

Probably the thought of how big a fool I was about to make of myself.

I was walking around by the starting blocks, trying not to limp, when Rooster Andrews asked what was the matter with me. Rooster was the starter. He had started me in any number of races and probably officiated at more track and field meets and other athletic events than anybody in Texas. I think he was fond of me because we both shared athletic handicaps. He had overcome his (being only five feet tall) to play football at the University of Texas. I was still suffering with mine—an erratic coordination that always seemed to strike me when I least needed it. I told him nothing was the matter.

He said, "Well, you act like you are limping." I told him that, no, I was just practicing being light on my feet, trying to walk without letting them touch the ground, and right then I was working on my left foot. He said he'd never heard of such a training method, but that it just might work.

Coach Rogers's rap on me was that I didn't sprint between the hurdles. This was especially true of the highs but didn't hurt me so badly in the lows. Apparently, the greater distance between hurdles in the lows gave my brain more time to communicate with my legs and tell them, "O.K., you're over the hurdle. Now the idea is to run like hell until you get to the next one."

Or something like that.

It came time to get down in the blocks. My heart was going like a trip-hammer. Gone was any hope of making the finals, much less placing. All I wanted to do was finish the race. If I didn't, if I had to limp off the track, the coach was going to examine me and find the blister. And what would I tell him then? That I had stepped on top of the kitchen stove? That I had been striking matches with my toes? I sure as hell wasn't going to tell him the truth. If I did, I would be known as Candlefoot the rest of my days at Bay City.

Rooster called, "Set!" and an instant later the gun went off. I don't remember much about the first part of the race. All I knew was that I was springing off that left foot, trying to limit its time on the ground to the smallest possible duration, and racing like hell to the next hurdle so I could get it up in the air for a brief instant of relief before I had to snap it back down and drive for the next hurdle. I wasn't even aware of how fast I was running. It didn't even begin to occur to me until I cleared the last hurdle and was on my way to the finish line. That's when I noticed, for the first time, that unlike my usual races, nobody was in front of me. I hit the tape a clear winner by ten yards.

I coasted a few steps and veered off onto the infield grass and just stopped. I was scared to take another step. Coach Rogers came running up to me, and he was ecstatic. "Boy," he said, "that's what I been trying to teach you! Sprint between those hurdles! Boy, you did it today!"

I mumbled something about how it must have been the energy I got from the Hershey bar.

He said, "Well, whatever it was, you keep it up. Now cool out. Jog around."

Of course, I didn't. As soon as the coach was off somewhere else I started to make my way out of the stadium as unobtrusively as I could. But before I could get to the gate, I caught the tail end of what the P.A. announcer was saying: ". . . a new Black Cat Relays record in the 180-yard low hurdles. Nineteen-point-six seconds."

The crowd started to applaud, and Rooster came over and clapped me on the back. "That's the way to go! Congratulations." I made some reply and started toward the parking lot, still wearing my spikes and warmups. I didn't dare go in the locker room to change. Rooster watched me for a few steps and said, "Still practicing walking without your feet touching the ground?" "Just about," I said.

The finals weren't until that afternoon, so I went home to survey the damage. It was bad. The blister, now about the size of a silver dollar, looked like a piece of raw calf's liver. I was pretty melancholy. Here I had just set my first and only track record (I had never before broken 21 seconds in the event), and I probably wouldn't be able to run in the finals.

Fortunately, my mother was out when I reached home, so I got out the pan again and set to work with the water, salt and iodine. But I knew it was a lost cause, because I had only about three hours before the finals, and the foot was worse than it had been the night before.

I ran the race, mainly because I couldn't think of a good way to get out of it, but I would rather not tell you too much about that. The part I remember best was between the third and fourth hurdles. Coach Rogers was at the side of the track yelling at me, "You're not running! You're not running!" Which was true, but I wasn't limping either. I had about an inch-thick pad of bandages on my foot, which wasn't doing anything to improve my style or my coordination.

I finished last. When the race was over I went out to the middle of the infield and sat down, trying to figure how I was going to get out of the stadium and to my home.

Coach Rogers came over and said, "What in the world was the matter with you? You looked like you were running on one leg. Where was that guy who ran this morning?" I mumbled something about him forgetting to give me a Hershey bar. He turned around in disgust. "Oh, the dickens! A Hershey bar wouldn't have made that much difference. Good grief! Hershey bar!"

I said, "Well, it was psychological."

"Psychological! You don't even know what the word means! Psychological, my foot!" And he turned around and walked off. I could see by the set of his neck he wasn't real happy with me. I wanted to call after him, "Yes, it was my foot. Psychological or not!" After a while Rooster came over and squatted down by me and asked what was the matter. He said, "And don't tell me any more of that stuff about walking around without your feet touching the ground."

Well, I had to tell somebody, and Rooster was a good guy. I knew he wouldn't spread it around, so I took off my shoe and showed him. I also swore him to secrecy and told him the whole story. He asked what explanation I had given to Coach Rogers. When I told him, he nodded and said, "I guess it was psychological. On your part anyway."

I didn't know quite what he meant.

He said, "You know, you aren't the first track man who ever got a blister the day before a race. They got stuff that will take care of that. If you had called the coach last night, or even come in early this morning, they could have treated it with something like Tuf-Skin and you could have run . You ought not to have tried to hide it. Coach Rogers wouldn't have told anybody."

So there you are, young athletes. It pays to be honest and forthright. Deceit might get you through the prelims, but it will never last through the finals.

4

It Wasn't a
Real Big Lie

Actually it was a double lie. As you'll read I had been, for many years, telling a lie about my tryout with the St. Louis Cardinals baseball team and how I was offered a contract. In the story you're going to read I didn't get offered a contract, which was the lie I'd been telling for all those years.

But later I was actually offered a minor-league contract, probably to be assigned to the Columbus, Georgia, team of the, I think, Southern League. This happened around 1954. I'd been playing football that season at Blinn Junior College in Brenham, Texas, and I wasn't doing much good. In those days, and at the colleges where I was playing, they weren't throwing the ball. In fact I think a hell of a lot more passes were made in the stands than we threw on the field.

Mostly we blocked and tackled. Now, at 190 pounds I was big enough, but I just wasn't all that charmed with wrestling around with those big linebackers and tackles. I wanted to get out and get loose and catch the ball and do a little free-lance running.

But that didn't look like it was going to happen. My ambition had been to play in the Southwest Conference, and, toward that end, I'd done my apprenticeship at three junior colleges. Except nothing came of it. I'd had a tryout at Baylor, the passingest school around, but I'd managed to acquire a stress fracture of my shin bone about the third day in early camp.

Cancel that one out.

So at the end of the season at Blinn I'd applied to be received into the Aviation Cadet program of the U.S. Air Force. I'd passed the written and physical tests and been told to go home and wait.

So I'd gone back to Bay City, Texas, to hang around and await orders.

Now at this point I hadn't been sworn in. They screen aviation-cadet candidates pretty thoroughly and, while I was waiting, the FBI was busy checking into my background to see if I was subversive or merely confused.

About that time they announced they were holding another Cardinal tryout camp in Houston. It was March and I was bored and I thought, what the hell. I'd been playing a little semi-pro ball in the Rice Belt League and I was fairly sharp so I thought I'd go down and give it a try. After all, I was nearly three years older than when I'd first tried out as a green seventeen-year-old. Maybe maturity would help. I'd heard my mother use the word in application to myself, but I didn't know what it meant. Maybe it meant I'd finally be able to solve the puzzle of the curve ball.

So I went down there and had a good tryout. The upshot was that they took me up to the offices in old Buff Stadium and Johnny Keane sat down to tell me about the deal. Keane had been the manager of the Houston Buffaloes when I had been their most ardent fan. He was now a scout for the Cardinals and I was more than a little impressed. Hell, I felt like Mickey Mantle. I could see my future unfolding before me like a giant panorama of the American Dream.

Then Keane started talking. There was no mention of a signing bonus. I wasn't of that caliber. He finally got down to the hard points of the case and it turned out that they'd be willing to pay me $150 a month during the season and during spring training.

He also promised me a lot of long bus trips.

So much for the Mickey Mantle syndrome. Reality set in.

I asked him how far he thought I could go and he was candid. Now this was back in the days when they didn't pay .220 hitters a ton a year. Keane said he doubted I'd ever go much further than double-A ball and I might not even reach that, but they had a farm system they needed to keep filled and if I wanted it I could have it.

Well, I had the speed and I could field my position at third base even if I had to use most of my anatomy to do it. And I could throw.

But I wasn't knocking down any fences with my bat.

It was fun, I got to tell you. There I was, sitting at a desk in the offices of a professional baseball team, a contract in front of me, and one of my childhood idols sitting beside me with a pen. Listen, that can turn any nineteen-year-old's head. At that age the idea of somebody asking me what I did and being able to say, somewhat loftily, "I'm a professional baseball player," was a dream I'd been dreaming ever since I'd got my first Marty Marion signature glove.

While I was sitting there deliberating, Mr. Keane had said, "Son, I'll tell you straight. You just don't get around on the ball fast enough. You're a big strong kid, but you don't have the wrists. And you've got a pretty good arm, but it's not a major-league arm. But you make up your own mind."

I did. At that time the Air Force was paying Aviation Cadets $120 a month and that included room and board and no bus trips. Plus it was year round.

I said, "Johnny . . ."

At least I got that much out of it, calling one of my idols by his first name.

I said, "Johnny, the Air Force pays better and I don't have to stop line drives with my face."

I left. Turned them down. Walked away. Stole home.

So, you see, it wasn't a real big lie.

The other night, talking to my wife, Betsyanne, I made passing reference to the time I was offered a contract by the St. Louis Cardinals to sign with their Columbus, Georgia, farm team. I reckon I've told that story three or four hundred times, and 10 seconds after I made the remark, I realized what a lie it was.

The only thing is, I'm not sure how *big* a lie it was on account of Duane Dean's daddy's 1948 Mercury. Now that may seem a little obscure, but it has to do with why I've felt entitled to tell that lie all these years.

Back in the early '50s I was a senior in high school in Bay City, Texas, and the starting third baseman and leadoff hitter for the baseball team. I was told, on a number of occasions, that I was the slickest-fielding infielder that the school had ever had and, on general principles, I agreed with that assessment. The fact that Coach Don Haley seemed to disagree in no way made me believe less of myself. He once told me, "Son, I think I'll just stick up a post down there by third base. That way the ball has a chance of hitting it and might stop. At least the post won't jump out of the way."

But to get back to the Cardinals and the contract and Duane Dean's daddy's 1948 Mercury. We were headed for a baseball tournament in Cuero, Texas, and we had word that an actual scout for the Cardinals was going to be there. Well, I don't know where you grew up, or where you played your ball (if you did, I bet you hit .190 and couldn't have gotten around second base if you were riding a Cushman motor scooter), but in my part of Texas the thought that there was going to be a Cardinal scout at a tournament you were playing in was enough to cause you to give up girls and Hershey bars for a solid week.

There was also word around that the scout was going to be looking especially hard at the Bay City team, which automatically convinced me he was really interested in its premier third baseman. Coach Haley's opinion notwithstanding, besides being a good fielder, I was a good hitter. By that point in the season I was hitting pretty close to .400 and I could run. I had gone to the state meet in the high hurdles and had run at least one wind-aided 100-yard dash just a tad under 10 flat. And I could slide.

Even Coach Haley agreed with me on that. We were playing the Wharton High School team and he was talking to their coach while I was standing nearby. He said, "Yeah, I only got one guy who can slide"—and he jerked his thumb at me—"but he can't get on base."

Which wasn't true. Coach Haley was always riding me, trying to unnerve me and shake my confidence. It never worked, though, because I knew the coach knew that I had the talent to make it big. The constant teasing and derision was just to keep me from getting a swelled head and to keep me on my toes. So I couldn't agree with something he subsequently said. I got on base a lot by getting hit with pitched balls, and Coach Haley made the remark that, while my ability to get hit in the head by a pitched ball and take my base helped the team, it certainly did nothing for my scholastic record. He even went on to say that he figured if I got hit in the head by enough pitched balls I'd make an excellent politician. Which was a lie. I've never been elected to a single office in my life.

But that was Coach Haley for you.

And when I tell you what he did to me when we were going to that tournament in Cuero, you'll understand how he could have made those other unkind remarks about me.

The team traveled on a bus, but Coach Haley always drove his car and he usually picked out two or three of the players to go with him. For some reason he very often picked me to go in his car.

The trip to Cuero was no exception.

It wasn't so bad for most of the way. Our really good catcher, Duane Dean, was in the front seat, and me and the shortstop,

Buddy Barrett, were in back. About ten miles from Cuero, Coach Haley looked in the rearview mirror and said, "Son, I think I'm going to play you in right field."

I didn't say a word because I figured he was talking to Barrett. But then Barrett didn't say anything, so I said, "Sir?"

And he said, "Yeah, and I'm going to hit you eighth in the lineup."

The man was actually talking to *me*. And he was talking about putting the slickest-fielding infielder in Bay City High School history in right field.

He was actually talking about putting the fastest man on the team in the lowest spot in the lineup—with a St. Louis Cardinal scout in the stands.

Good God, if we hadn't been going 60 miles an hour I'd of bailed out right there and hitchhiked home.

Well, he carried me along with that story right up until he made out the lineup card, which was where I saw I'd been restored to my rightful position. I challenged him right then: I said, "Why'd you tell me you wasn't going to start me at third base?"

He said, "I wasn't. But the post didn't show up and I didn't have nobody else."

Well, it doesn't matter how I did during the tournament. You wouldn't believe me anyway if I told you how well I played. But after the last game we were in the dressing room, and Coach Haley come up and said, "I don't know why anybody would want to see you two mudheads, but there's a man in my office wants to talk to you."

He was speaking to me and Duane Dean, who'd also had a pretty good tournament.

Well, we went to the office in the high school gymnasium and there was a guy wearing a white shirt, with a cigar stuck between his teeth. He said, "Hello, boys, I'm a scout for the St. Louis Cardinal organization and we'd like to invite you to Houston for a tryout."

Well, good grief, I know how blasé athletes are today, but that was back when every high school ballplayer could tell you Ted Williams' and Stan Musial's and even Junior Gilliam's batting average. I mean, the man had just said a tryout, a real tryout, with the St. Louis Cardinal organization.

We drove back to Bay City in a slight state of euphoria. Or at least Duane Dean and I did. Barrett wasn't saying anything because he hadn't been offered a tryout with the Cardinals, and Coach Haley just kept shaking his head and making remarks about what the state of professional baseball had finally come to.

That tryout camp was about a month off, and I reckon that was the longest month I've ever spent in my life. I fielded ground balls and line drives and pop-ups during, before and after practice. I practiced as long as the light held out and as long as I could find somebody to hit to me.

Man, I was ready. I even went to bed every night with a ball tied up in my glove to try to improve the pocket.

Well, the day finally came, and Duane and I loaded up his daddy's 1948 Mercury and set off for Houston. We were going to stay with my Aunt Sylvia during the three days of the tryout (they hadn't offered us any expense money), which was to be at old Buff Stadium, the home of the world-famous Houston Buffaloes, winners of the 1947 Dixie Series.

I want to state here and now that I'm not going to tell you much about that tryout. The reason I'm not is that some of the details are still a little too painful. There must've been about a hundred guys who showed up the first day. The coaches in charge put us through timed sprints and infield drills and controlled batting practice and all that sort of stuff.

There I was standing on the same infield where Tommy Glaviano and Billy Costa and Solly Hemus had played, and in the outfield had been Eddie Knoblauch and Hal Epps. It hadn't been much more than five years since I'd sat up in those very stands, eating hot dogs and hamburgers and watching those same ball-players on the very field I was standing on. I mean, my spikes were sunk in the very same dirt theirs had been.

Well, I survived that first day. The way they did it was to post a list of the players they wanted back the next day and, when the list was posted, my name was among those thirty-odd players they were inviting back.

Heck, I was on Easy Street that night in my Aunt Sylvia's house. I could already see myself wearing that Cardinal uniform and maybe giving fielding tips to Marty Marion. The only thing in my way was a little bit of time.

Now, at this point, I have to tell you about one slight defect I had as a player: I didn't really have the great arm. Coach Haley and I were in agreement on that point.

In fact, he was once so unkind as to ask me why I didn't go ahead and donate it to the Salvation Army. I asked him what he meant, and he said, "Ain't you ever seen those donation boxes? That's where you're supposed to put your old rags."

But he said something worse to me. One time we were taking infield practice and I'd just made a throw to first base when he came walking onto the field shaking his head and saying, "No, no, no." He came up to me and took me by the shoulder and said, "Son, don't throw the ball to first base. Carry it over there. That way it'll get there sooner and we can be sure it will arrive. It will also be a lot less dangerous for the people in the stands behind first base."

Which was a damn lie, because I'd never hit anybody in those stands yet.

But this time I was determined. I wasn't just snapping my wrist on those infield throws, I was snapping my ankles. I'd figured I didn't have a thing to lose; that this time it was do or die and I wasn't saving anything back. I wasn't just putting myself behind those throws, I was putting my parents and my grandparents and their parents before them.

I remember that, at the end of the workout on the second day, they were having us bring it home Duane Dean was the catcher because by then he'd established himself as the premier athlete on the field, which he was. Well, I was socking that ball in there. I made four throws in a row at ankle height without Duane having to move his glove an inch. But I damn near threw my back out in the process.

Anyway, I thought I was a made man. At that point I was figuring on a year in the minors at the very most.

Then I read the board. And my name wasn't on it. I wasn't being invited back another day. I was through.

Duane Dean couldn't believe it. I told him I'd go ahead and take the bus back to Bay City. I didn't want to stick around and be humiliated any worse. He insisted, however, on the two of us talking to one of the coaches who was running the camp. Well, I was kind of embarrassed, but we went on over and talked to this coach who was leaning up against the wall in front of the box seats. Old Duane wanted to know why I'd been cut. He claimed I'd fielded and hit and run about as well as anyone. But the coach said they were worried about my arm, that I didn't really have the great arm. Well, Duane protested that, pointing out those great throws I'd made to home plate. The coach kind of glanced at me and then he put his arm around Duane's shoulders and they walked away a few feet. I reckoned they were trying to get to where I couldn't hear them, but that wasn't the way it worked out. The coach said, "Son, the reason we cut him is that we don't need no one-armed infielders in the St. Louis Cardinal chain."

And Duane said, "What are you talking about?"

The coach said, "What I mean is, if he keeps throwing like he throws now it ain't going to be too long until he's got just that one arm."

Which wound up my tryout with the Cardinals.

But I've got a point to make. As we get older we tend to remember how much faster we ran the 100-yard dash and how many more touchdowns we scored in the big game or how many hits we got in a season.

So old age is creeping up on all of us. And none of us can run a 9.6 hundred anymore, or catch three touchdown passes from W.C. Gosling anymore. Or remember all the fights we thought we'd won in all those tin-roofed dance halls we were in when we were rodeoing.

Or all those contracts we signed with the St. Louis Cardinals.

But I want to ask for a fair assessment of the lie I've been telling for twenty-eight years. It is a fact that Duane Dean and I were invited to the Cardinal tryout camp. And it's a fact that, out of the hundred players invited, Duane Dean did get offered a contract by the Cardinals, even though he threw it over for a college scholarship.

I didn't get offered a contract. I got cut on the second day.

But I did ride down to that tryout camp in Duane Dean's daddy's 1948 Mercury. And we did stay at my Aunt Sylvia's house during those tryouts.

And, not only that, I rode back to Bay City, Texas, in the same 1948 Mercury that I'd come up there in, and the guy who was driving it had a signed offer in his pocket from the St.Louis Cardinals.

If that, right there, does not entitle you to go around lying the rest of your life that you were offered a contract by the St. Louis Cardinals, then there is something wrong with this democracy!

You can't get much closer.

5

The Great Fourth of July Donkey Baseball Game

Everybody wants to be wanted, to be selected, to be sought. That's happened to me about twice in my life. Once was on the occasion of this story, the other time was back in my rodeo days when two of the ugliest girls I've ever seen were fighting over me in some honky-tonk outside of Fort Smith, Arkansas. I think they both went on to become professional wrestlers.

But the facts documented in the following piece were no joke, especially for a slow-thinking teenager who was in awe of anybody over the rank of Sunday School teacher.

As you'll read, this was a donkey baseball game with the police department against the firemen. They took it deadly serious as you'll no doubt surmise. I have mentioned in the story how the police chief approached me, but I never got to how the fire chief scared the liver out of me after I'd defected. Now this won't sound like much in this day and age of communication, but you have to remember that I was a very impressionable boy of slack years who tended to believe anything anyone over the age of twenty told me. And when the fire chief came to me and asked, darkly, if I realized that boys my age could be drafted into the fire department just as they could be drafted into the Army, I tended to believe him.

And it scared the hell out of me.

Though I have been guilty of exaggerations in the past and will probably be again in the future, there are none such in this story. If anything I am guilty of under-exaggeration.

Especially when it comes to how mean that devil mule was. Since that afternoon when I was partially on his back, I have come to judge people and situations in accordance with the meanness of that mule.

I have never found, and that includes my second wife, anything to match it.

When I was growing up in the late 1940s, people in small towns in Texas and other parts of the South didn't have quite as many diversions as they do today. There were not as many TV sets; the movie theaters changed their films only on occasion; and not everybody and his teenager had a car. People were obviously looking for other ways to have fun.

That's about the only reason I can think of for anyone to play donkey baseball—a little-known addendum to the Great American Pastime that had its heyday about the time I was graduating from high school.

For the uniniated, donkey baseball is baseball played while riding donkeys—the game we all know with a few additional rules. You could get off your donkey to field a ground ball or to catch a fly, but you had to bat, the pitcher had to pitch and the catcher had to catch while astride the critters.

Now there may be people—such as little girls in black patent-leather shoes and frilly dresses who haven't got time for such things, or misers who haven't finished counting their money, or preachers with the sins of the world to consider—who don't like baseball. There may be an embittered third baseman somewhere who has failed his tryout with the Cardinals and never wants to hear the game mentioned again; or there may be a baseball Scrooge who could put Ebenezer to shame.

But those attitudes are nothing but the last faint flickering glimmer of a long-dead star to the way a donkey feels about the game.

I can tell you flat-out that donkeys don't like baseball. They don't like to listen to it on the radio; they don't like to watch it; and, above all, they don't like to play it. A donkey's reaction to a baseball coming his way is "When is the next bus leaving town?" And he'll try to depart at that instant to be at the station early.

But given the level of baseball we used to play in Bay City, Texas, we had to do something to draw a crowd to the ball field. So we made donkey baseball an annual affair, played on the Fourth of July, with the police battling the fire department. The only problem with this game was that neither the police department nor the fire department was heavily populated with athletes. Some of the participants, as a matter of fact, were getting a little long in the tooth and had the same attitude toward baseball that the donkeys did. Consequently, both teams recruited athletes from the high school. This involved a good deal of skulduggery, since the rules said that all players had to be members in good standing of their respective organizations.

I was on the high school baseball team and I also rodeoed, and while I wasn't particularly good at either sport, the combination was a natural for donkey baseball, automatically making me a popular draft choice.

In 1952, the fire chief found me hanging around the town square. He came up to me, put his hand on my shoulder and said, "Son, you like chicken-fried steak, don't you?"

Well, I admitted I did, though it was an unnecessary question because there wasn't a high school boy in Texas who didn't like chicken-fried steak.

Now, there's a myth circulating around in the North, the East, and other depressed areas that chili is the national dish of Texas. That is not so. Chicken-fried steak is. As a matter of fact, one of the reasons that Texas athletes are bigger and taller and faster than most others from less fortunate states is because of the nutritional value of chicken-fried steak, a commodity that male Texans begin eating at the age of one.

Next he said, "And you like cherry pie, don't you?"

I said I sure did.

"With a glass of cold milk?"

I guaranteed him that was a fact. "Well," he said, "I don't know who it was done it, since I know it'd be against the rules to try and bribe an interscholastic-league high school baseball player, but somebody has left a $25 credit down at the Texan Cafe for you, and that ought to buy a whole bunch of chicken-fried steak and milk and cherry pie."

As any nutritionist knows, you add cherry pie and milk to your natural base of chicken-fried steak and you've got a dynamite package. I would hazard a guess that any Texas high-school athlete who trains on $25 worth, given prices in those days, would not only be able to perform incredible athletic feats, but would be able to do them while riding not just a donkey, but any other four-footed animal you could name, including a bobcat.

Well, he had my attention, so I nodded when he said, "Can we expect you out at practice next week?"

Now all these deals were supposed to be kept top secret, but somehow the word always got out. Next day the police chief came by the house to see me.We got settled in the living room and he asked what I was going to be doing on the Fourth of July.

I think I told him that I had to go visit my grandmother or that I needed to take the radio in to Houston to get it fixed, as we'd been having trouble getting *Amos 'n' Andy* of late.

He just gave me a kind of thoughtful, sorrowful look and went to pulling papers out of his pocket. He said, "Well, I just happened to notice these tickets you've got in our files. Looks like about two speeding tickets and several parking tickets and here's one for running a red light. Now I know these must have slipped your mind or else you'd already have paid them."

And he gave me that sorrowful look again.

"So what I'll do," he said, "is I'll just take these on down to the Justice of the Peace so as to save you a trip and you can drop by there and pay them. Like tomorrow."

Well, I did some fast arithmetic and I knew those tickets were going to cost more than $25 worth of chicken-fried steak. So I cleared my throat and asked him what that date was again.

He said, gently, "The Fourth of July. Remember? Independence Day? Fireworks? Parades? Donkey baseball?"

I told him it was all coming back to me and I must have got my calendar mixed up because I wasn't doing anything about that time. He said that was just fine and got up, leaving the tickets on the couch. Just as he went out the door he said, "Can we expect you at practice?"

I told him absolutely, without fail.

So I became a member of the police force—or, I should say, the mounted police.

Well, naturally, I kind of avoided the fire chief after my sudden switch of allegiance. I quit hanging around the square, and I quit answering the telephone. At one point my mother asked me why the fire chief kept calling me. I acted innocent and told her I didn't know, but she still gave me a pretty suspicious look and wanted to know what kind of trouble I'd gotten myself into with the fire department. It seemed that whenever anyone in authority was looking for me, my mother was pretty well convinced they weren't trying to pass along the news that I'd just won an academic scholarship—an attitude that weakened my confidence.

Another problem was that there weren't enough donkeys to go around. So they had to substitute a few mules. Now on the surface that seems an innocent enough statement, "substitute a few mules." Well, the way a donkey feels about baseball ain't shucks to the way a mule feels. In fact, I think you could say that a mule almost lines up with the Communist Party in his attitude toward the Great American Pastime.

But of all the mules in Matagorda County the one that had to be considered the meanest was a big, blue-lipped devil named Anse that belonged to the Purvis brothers. The Purvises were two old recluse bachelors who lived outside of town. For years it had been their habit to come into town on a Saturday morning driving a wagon pulled by that mule. The mule would generally do all right until he got to the little wooden bridge across Caney Creek, on the outskirts of town. There he would stop, and no power on earth could budge him. The Purvis brothers finally got in the habit of carrying a little kindling, and when the mule stopped, they'd get out and build a fire under him. But to show you how devious and ornery that mule was, on several occasions he'd go forward just enough to get the wagon over the fire. He succeeded in charring the wagon more than once.

Anse was the mount I drew, and as far as I was concerned, he was three or four times meaner than Attila the Hun.

July Fourth came and, as was traditional, things began with a parade right after a picnic. The parade would end at the ball field; we'd have the game; and then there would be a fireworks display and free watermelon.

Both teams marched in the parade, some players riding their mounts, other, less confident ones leading them. We made a brave sight in our uniforms, though with one incongruous note: donkey baseball is probably the only sport in which the players wear spurs taped to their spikes.

There was the usual argument when both chiefs turned in their lineup cards to Mayor Gusman, the home-plate umpire. The fire chief, noting the name of a high school athlete, said, "Now wait a minute, this boy's not a member of the police force. Hell, he's still in high school!"

And the police chief said, "No, he came to us last year and evinced a great ambition to be a policeman, so we started an apprentice program for him. But you should talk. Here's this kid Barrett, and I know for a fact the closest he ever came to a fire was roasting a hot dog over one."

It went on like that until Mayor Gusman said, "Oh, shut up. I ought to disqualify you both for being such poor liars, but all these people have paid money to see the bunch of you make fools of yourself and I don't want to disappoint 'em. Play ball!"

The fire chief acted kind of hurt at me. The whole fire department, for that matter, was none too kind. A few of them even whispered "sellout" and "traitor." I thought that was a little mean, them not knowing the true circumstances.

We played pretty even up to the third inning, when we lost our best hitter, Bobby White. He hit a sharp single to center field, but going down the line to first base, his donkey shied and ran headlong into the bleacher fence, throwing Bobby up into the nickel seats and breaking his collarbone. They had a good deal of trouble running down the ball in the outfield, but they finally tagged White out just as he was being loaded into the ambulance.

But we got back at them in the fourth inning, when we put Barrett out of the game. In donkey baseball you don't brush the batter back, you brush his mount back, which is much more effective. But our pitcher slipped a little and caught Barrett's donkey in the ear with a slow curve. The result was that Barrett ended up in foul territory with a dislocated shoulder.

I was having my own troubles. This devil mule I'd drawn was big and he quickly learned that once I got down to field a ground ball, I was going to be encumbered by a glove and a ball when I tried to get back on to make my throw. Of course, none of us used a saddle; the last thing you wanted was to get tangled up in the stirrups. So I'd have to try and jump up on that mule's back, then swing my leg over. It was always at just that point that he'd decide to go rodeoing.

But the same was happening to most of the other players, and by the time the game was half over, we were all hot and disgusted and tired and ready to kill every donkey and mule in six states.

We got to the last of the ninth with the fire department leading 35–33. It appeared to be all over when our first two men were put out. But then we got our next two batters on, and I squibbed a little infield hit to the third baseman. Ordinarily I would've been out, but his donkey ran off just long enough for me to reach first base.

So there we were, with the bases loaded and two out. Our next batter hit a fly ball to center field. Now if the center fielder had gotten off his mount it would have been an easy out, but he decided to showboat and make the catch mounted. Just before he got to the ball he touched his donkey with his spurs, and the donkey, which was about as disgusted as the rest of us, picked that instant to go rodeoing. The ball fell free and we went dashing around the bases. Our man on third scored, our man on second scored and my mule and I were really flying. We rounded second and then third and were only 90 feet from victory. It looked so sure that a couple of the police had jerked a big piece of red, white and blue bunting off the face of the grandstand and stretched it out in front of the plate for me to ride over as I scored the winning run.

But they hadn't counted on that devil mule. Halfway between third and home he came to a dead stop. I kicked him, I spurred him, I whacked him with my glove, but that mule obviously thought home plate was the bridge at Caney Creek, and he wasn't going to move.

Well, it was a madhouse. The stands were yelling, my team was jumping up and down, they were still trying to run the ball down in the outfield and I didn't know what to do to get that mule going. Finally I noticed a friend of mine, Crook Adams, leaning against the little fence that ran down the third-base line. I yelled at him to throw me his lighter, and he tossed the big Zippo I knew he always carried. Well, I caught it, lit it up, and then leaned down and applied a good flame to that mule's belly.

For a second nothing happened. That devil mule just kind of switched his ears back and forth and mouthed his bit and shook his head. But then, just as I thought he'd catch fire, he began to move—and he moved at such a speed that I was barely able to hang on. We went straight through that banner. Right behind it was the catcher on his donkey, the pitcher on his donkey and Mayor Gusman on his donkey. That big mule and I hit them full tilt, and donkeys and pitcher and catcher and mayor went flying in all directions.

And if that wasn't enough confusion, the boys in charge of the fireworks decided it was time to set off the display. That was the last straw for a bunch of irritated, overheated, disgusted mules and donkeys. In about thirty seconds the playing field looked like Custer's Last Stand, with players lying all over the place.

Well, we finally got things calmed down, and the mayor, as mad as he was, declared my run valid, and we won the game 36–35. I thought that was it, and I was feeling pretty good until the fire chief, still looking hurt about my having run out on him, came up and wrote me out a citation for violating the city fire code: attempting to set fire to a mule in the midst of a public gathering.

Ever since, I've always considered it was just that sort of short-sighted thinking that kept donkey baseball from taking its place among the other major sports of our time.

6

The Bare Facts about Hazing

In 1964 and part of 1965, while I was learning to be a writer, I worked for the Clyde Wilson agency as a private investigator. During that period I spent part of my time on Clyde's cases and the other part trying to run down the upperclassmen who'd caused me such a skin-flaking desire to die. My plan was to find them, then put together a big enough bankroll to hire a gang of toughs to go to wherever they were and beat them up.

I never found them.

Dick Castleberry was my co-victim. I've also looked for Dick, but in vain. I reckon he died young, probably of chagrin.

If you're a sadist, read on.

I guess it was the broom drive, more than anything else, that really was responsible for the creation of Freshman Night at the Fort. This was back in the days right after the Korean war when I was playing football at John Tarleton Junior College in Stephenville, Texas. The Fort was an old, dilapidated former Army barracks that was used as the athletic dormitory. Tarleton State University is a four-year university now, but it is still part of the Texas A&M system, just as it was in 1952. The sort of hazing that had long been standard fare at A&M was practiced at Tarleton, too. Because we football players were supposedly tougher than the average students, hazing in the Fort was serious stuff.

Take the broom drive for example. When I checked into the dorm for preseason practice, the first thing I noticed was a big sign in the hall that said each freshman must keep a broom in his room at all times. "Oh, good," I thought, "Mom'll be so pleased. I'll be keeping my room neat and all that." Well, it wasn't until the afternoon that I found out the real purpose of that broom—and why Coach Sandy Sanford eventually would have to ask the seniors to hold off on us till the season was over. When a senior said, "Freshman, get your broom," you went to your room, collected your broom and took it down the hall to the bathroom and soaked it in the toilet until it felt like it weighed twenty or thirty pounds. Then you reported to the senior who was waiting for you in the hall. There was a line marked off across the hall, and you'd be told to "assume the position," which meant you toed the mark, bent down and grasped both your ankles. Then the senior would see how far he could drive you with one swat.

That was bad enough, but before long the seniors began competing to see who could drive a freshman the farthest. To even things up, they began giving out handicaps. I mean you wouldn't expect a little senior quarterback to be able to drive a big freshman tackle very far, and it wouldn't have been very fair for some big old tackle to have a small freshman halfback to flail away at, so the seniors carefully paired up the drivers and the drivees. Unfortunately, I was kind of caught in the middle. I was a 190-pound receiver and defensive back, and I'd also caught the attention of a very large offensive tackle, Jim Bomar, from Paragould, Arkansas. Bomar was pretty much the ringleader of the hazing and had decided he had dibs on me. "Boy, I like your height," he said. "And them long arms . So when I bust you I want you to reach out and get me all the distance you can. What I'm trying to tell you, boy, is I think you got the goods to make me the world broom-driving record holder." Well, there just ain't no disputing that kind of logic.

But I guess the worst part of it was when the seniors would have disputes over the measuring. You'd be lying there, stretched full out on the hall floor, your bottom ringing, and you'd hear the arguing begin. One driver would say, "I measured him at an even 8'11"." Then another would say, "Damned if that's so! Look where his fingers are curled back to now. Just take that tape measure. It ain't no more than 8'6"." You knew what was coming next: "Freshman, get back up here and assume the position." Bomar would say in an injured tone of voice, "By damn, I'll just show you guys. I'll stretch him out to an even nine foot this time!And you measure him quick, before his fingers start to curl. Let's keep in mind that the rules of the competition say to where his out-stretched fingers reach!"

But one day Coach Sanford called all the upperclassmen to-gether and told them that there were more freshmen getting hurt in the dorm than on the playing field. "Gentlemen," he said, "I'm going to make a deal with you. We're in the running for the conference championship and a bid to the Little Rose Bowl, but we can't make it if we get too many more injuries. So I want you guys to agree to lay off them freshmen until after the last game."

Well, we didn't make it to the Little Rose Bowl, and a week after our last game, Bomar got up during dinner, banged on an iced-tea pitcher to get our attention and said, "Well, boys, the night you've been waiting for is finally here. Right after you get through with your supper, go on back to the Fort and wait in your rooms. Don't rush, because we're going to give you time to digest your dinner. And you might try and catch a little nap. Might not get too much sleep tonight. But be sure and stay in your rooms until we get you out. If you come out before you're told to, you'll just be calling attention to yourself and that wouldn't be real smart."

Well, they left us waiting in the Fort for hours. Building up the suspense, I guess. Then, at about one in the morning, the fresh-men were divided into small groups and loaded into cars. Dick Castleberry, a freshman running back, and I were with four seniors, one of whom was Bomar. We took off down the highway. For a while we stuck to the main road, but pretty soon we started turning off on tiny side roads. Neither Castleberry nor I had the slightest idea what was coming, and the seniors weren't saying. Castleberry and I just kept giving each other apprehensive looks. After about an hour we pulled up on the side of a deserted road.

"Little late for a picnic, ain't it?" I asked.

Bomar said, "Well, I guess you two better get your clothes off."

"Say what?" Castleberry said.

Bomar told us again.

"You'll have to whip us first," I said.

And good old Jim, in a very friendly voice, said, "Well we can do that, too."

It was about that time I realized that Castleberry and I were in a real spot. We were both pretty fast and they were all big tackles, and we could've outrun them easy. But they'd maneuvered us so we were backed up to one side of the car and the four of them were in a semi-circle around us.

But the only chance we had was to run. I figured Castleberry was thinking the exact same thing, so I yelled "Go!" and headed for a hole between Bomar and the guy on his right, Harry Cannon. I was running lead blocker for Castleberry, so I give Cannon a shoulder, hoping to wedge him out a little, and then planned on bouncing over into Bomar. But Jim grabbed me and I went down. I felt Castleberry running up my back, but Cannon got him just as he started over the top. No gain on the play. We put up a brief scuffle, but it wasn't any use. Inside of ten minutes we were standing there naked and the seniors were wishing us good luck in getting back to the campus.

"Coach says football builds character, and we're just trying to do our part by giving y'all a little off-season training," Bomar called out as the car pulled away.

Lord it was cold—must have been around twenty-five degrees. We didn't have a real good idea where we were, and we were hardly dressed for traveling. I had to agree with Bomar; this was going to be a real character builder.

Castleberry and I started jogging. We didn't know where we were going, but anything was better than standing still. Finally after three or four miles we got lucky; we struck the main highway, and there, just to our left, was a sign that read: STEPHENVILLE, 41 MILES. That was good news, but we were still naked, freezing and forty-one miles from the Fort, with several towns to get through on the way back.

"Castleberry," I said, "we're in big trouble."

"Yeah," was all he said. He was shivering too hard to carry on a full conversation.

We started jogging toward Stephenville. I didn't miss my shoes much—my feet were pretty tough since I only wore shoes when absolutely necessary, anyway—but I sure missed all the other stuff I usually wore in winter. Fortunately, it was about 4 AM and there were no cars on the road. But, unfortunately, dawn was about three hours away, and unless we were going to set a world record for the forty-one-mile run we would be out on the road just plain naked when the sun came up. Our only consolation was in knowing there were twenty-three other naked freshmen running around the countryside. We hoped the law would take that into consideration and not be too harsh on us individually.

Well, we'd jogged for about an hour when we saw a farmhouse sitting pretty close to the highway. We jumped into the ditch alongside the road and reconnoitered the place just like we'd been taught to do in ROTC. "Castleberry, look there," I said. "Help is at hand."Out behind the house we could see clothes hanging on a line. Obviously this farm wife was either lazy or forgetful, and she'd left the family's duds out overnight. "We are saved," I said.

We sneaked up on that clothesline, moving so carefully you'd have thought our lives were at stake. The moon was up, and it was pretty light, but we were doing an outstanding job of infiltration when, with us only twenty yards from the clothesline, about eight dogs suddenly came boiling out from under the house barking their fool heads off. Castleberry and I both threw it into high gear, dashing under the line, the dogs at our heels, and grabbing at whatever we could reach. We swept on around the house and headed for the highway. Lights were already coming on in the house, but we fooled those dogs. Both of us could break ten-flat and those dogs had never chased anyone faster than a meter reader. We left them standing at the edge of their yard barking. After that we kicked it on up the highway and went a half mile in what must have been close to collegiate record time. Finally we tumbled off the highway and got down in the ditch to see what kind of clothes we'd come away with. Castleberry had got himself a pair of bib overalls. They might have been a little big, but at least they were passable.

Once I saw what I had, I tried to trade Castleberry out of those overalls. I offered him my radio, my girl friend, my undying gratitude, even a hundred dollars, which he knew I didn't have. But he wouldn't budge. "I'd rather be dead," he said, "than wear *that* back to Stephenville." I had come away with a lady's slip.

Well, it was nearly dawn, and a little traffic was beginning to show up on the highway. While I waited in the ditch, clad in my slip, Castleberry stood by the side of the road and tried to thumb us a ride. Finally, a farmer in a pickup truck stopped. I was grateful that he didn't take off when I came bounding out of the ditch. Instead he let us into the cab and, with me sitting in the middle, we started for Stephenville. He was an old man, a tobacco chewer, and the back of his truck was loaded with chickens he was taking to market. For a long time he didn't say anything. Every once in a while he'd roll down the window and spit. When he did, he'd cut his eyes around at me. I was drawn up in as tight a ball as I could get into, but I still felt worse than if I'd been naked. Finally he said, "What's that you got on there, boy?"

"It's a long T-shirt," I said.

He spit out the window. "No, it ain't. It's a chemise. My woman's got a bunch just like it."

After that he said, "You be some of them college boys, ain't you?"

I said we were, and he said, "I told the old woman you were all crazy." He stopped there, not bothering to add, "And this proves it." But, then, he didn't have to.

Well, that old farmer turned out to be a lifesaver. He took us right to the steps of the Fort. The last thing he said was, "Sonny, I wouldn't be running around in them kind of clothes as a regular thing."

I thought we were home free and that I wouldn't be seen. But when we raced into the dorm, we found everyone up just about to go to breakfast.

I regretted our unfortunate timing for a long while. But looking back on it, I guess I didn't have it too rough. I finally got used to be calling Slip. I even got used to be calling Underwear and being shown ads in ladies' magazines and asked my preference. I didn't even mind when I got asked to dance a few times by some of the other jocks. I guess the worst cut was when one of the sororities invited me to appear in their fashion show.

I transferred to Del Mar Junior College in Corpus Christi, Texas, at the end of the semester. I knew there were people who'd say I was trying to run away from my reputation as a lingerie model, but that had nothing to do with it. Del Mar was trying to build a football program, and they were treating players more kindly than Tarleton was. The fact that there was a lot of enthusiastic talk about having another Freshman Night at the Fort didn't influence my decision one bit.

7

The Oldest Guy Off Campus with a New Letter Sweater

I don't know why I got involved in this silliness. Maybe I didn't have anything better to do at the time. Lord knows I can't explain it. Maybe I just did it for the money. That's as good an excuse as I can think of. Maybe you can figure it out—I sure can't.

When Blinn College gave me my football letter sweater twenty-eight years after I won it, I never thought it was going to cause me so much trouble. If I had, I guarantee you I would have turned it down.

Like all old athletes, I get stronger and faster in memory every year. And I will admit that I might have stretched a point or two in the past when telling about some incidents in my athletic career. Every once in a while I've been a little slippery about just how good I was. Nothing overt, but occasionally I've let fall remarks like, "Yeah, I doubled in the ninth inning and a couple of runners got home, which was all we needed." Or, "I was running the third leg of the mile relay and when I got the baton we weren't but ten yards down so that wasn't that much distance to make up."

Slick, right?

Well, they say all chickens come home to roost and mine finally came home when Blinn College gave me my letter sweater two years ago. I'd been semi-lying about my athletic prowess all through my middle age, but I did have one truth I was proud of.

And I'll be danged if that wasn't the one I got accused of lying about.

Blinn is a small junior college in Brenham, Texas. It's known for its good-looking girls and the high caliber of education it tries to impart. I'd played there in 1953, as an offensive end and a defensive halfback. We weren't any big deal; we had a following of about nine people, six of whom were related to the players. But anytime you're playing college football and you stick your head in a Riddell and pull up your socks, you'd better not walk out on that field unless you're ready to have the lunch knocked out of you.

I started all eight games for Blinn that season but left before the year was out to answer my country's call and help out the Air Force. Consequently, I wasn't there for the awards banquet and didn't get my letter sweater.

Well, I guess Blinn could have handled the guilt of having one of its ex-athletes running around without his letter sweater, but it happened that I had occasion to take a couple of high school football players up there for a tryout and I got to talking to the present coach, Ben Boehnke, and I sort of mentioned that I'd done a pretty good job for them and I'd never even seen a thread of a letter sweater.

The reason I wanted that letter sweater so bad was that I'd scored the winning touchdown—the only touchdown of my college career—against Victoria Junior College, and I was proud of it.

And that's the story I got accused of distorting at the letter sweater ceremony, in the office of Blinn President James Atkinson. I got to admit they done it up grand. Lord, they had everybody there—press, photographers, everybody.

I guess I got carried away, and before I knew it I'd told about beating Victoria in the first game of the '53 season. Now, Victoria Junior College was no joke. It was located in Victoria, Texas, a city at least twice the size of Brenham. The Victoria Pirates played in a separate conference, one made up of schools with more access to talent than tiny Blinn. Although our '52 record looked a little better than theirs, it didn't take into account the caliber of the teams we had each played during our regular schedule. Not to take anything away from my fellow Buccaneers, but I don't think we could have beaten New Mexico Body and Fender University if they'd spotted us two touchdowns.

But for some reason we got it together for that game. Maybe it was because we didn't want Victoria to think of us as "chump of the week," and have them yawning on the other side of the scrimmage line. Though their team was considered far above ours, we still planned to show up for the game and introduce them to the ferocity of the underdog. I think it was the John Wayne movie that pumped us all up. We'd gotten into town about two hours early. Well, what do you do with thirty football players? Leave them sitting on the bus? So Frank Butler, who was the coach then, somehow managed to find the owner of a movie theater in town and he opened up and showed us a film. It was *Red River*, and when it was over we all walked out in the fall sunshine feeling big and tough and slapping each other on the shoulder.

Earlier that year, I'd broken my right shinbone rodeoing, and when we were in the dressing room the trainer was taping a protective covering on it, and Tommy Cuba, our good tackle, looked over and said, "You better take that off. All you're doing is giving them a target to shoot at."

I ripped that tape loose and threw it in the corner. We were that fired up.

We played them off their feet. I took a lick on that right leg in the third quarter and had to be carried off the field. My mother was there and she nearly went into cardiac arrest because she didn't know what was the matter with me. I was back on the field two plays later. We were that fired up.

Going into the fourth quarter they were leading 7–6. We'd missed the PAT. Getting arrogant, the Pirates tried to drive on us instead of simply hanging on to the ball and running the clock down. With two minutes to go they fumbled on their own 40 and we recovered. From there we drove the ball down to their 9, where we stalled. Bobby Lynch, our fullback, punched it into the line for no gain and then Shorty McGinty, a really good halfback, had two tries at them, but it did us no good.

L.M. Killough, our quarterback, called time and went over to the sidelines to talk to Coach Butler. I'd gone over to the sidelines myself. I was standing just a few yards from where Coach Butler and L.M. were conferring. I had my helmet pushed back and I was getting a drink of water when I heard the coach say to L.M., "Throw the ball to Giles."

Well, what that remark did was send a shiver through my soul. To begin with, Giles didn't want the responsibility of catching the pass that meant victory or defeat. Secondly, I'd noticed that the

Victoria players were getting a little irritated about this bunch of upstarts trying to steal a game from them.

When that time-out wound down, we came back into the huddle and L.M. looked over at me and said, "It's on you."

If there'd been a bus out of town, I'd of taken it.

We hadn't completed four passes that day. But when it's fourth-and-goal from the nine with not much time and you've failed on three running plays, what are you going to do? We didn't have much of a field-goal kicker, either.

We *did* have a little jump pass. L.M. would take the snap, leap up in the air and try to hit me, cutting across the middle, or Henry Pearson, our right end.

When we came to the set position all I was praying for was that L.M. would throw to Henry.

I guess Victoria knew what we had to do. At the snap I took two steps off the line and cut toward the middle. The linebackers were already falling back so I was able to get underneath them. My next memory was seeing L.M. up in the air with the ball cocked behind his head in his right hand.

He was looking straight at me.

Then I saw the ball aimed at me. I kept waiting for a hand to come out and deflect it, but none did. The next thing I knew, it was cradled in my arms. I instinctively turned upfield.

After that everything kind of turned into slow motion. I caught the ball on about the five. I saw people coming at me, but I somehow evaded them. I remember crossing that broad stripe and punching it into the end zone.

That's the story I told at the letter-sweater presentation, and it went over very well.

The next morning at the motel this young reporter from Brenham's *Banner-Press* called me and said that he'd gone back in the files and that the game report didn't read anything like that.

I ain't real good in the mornings to begin with, and I believe a call like that would shake up a conservative banker.

I said, "Whaaat?"

He said, "The game account says that Bobby Lynch broke through the middle for 26 yards to score the winning touchdown."

Well, there wasn't a whole bunch I could say at that point.

But I brooded about it. I wouldn't even wear the letter sweater because I felt like it had been tarnished. Besides, have you ever seen anything sillier than a middle-aged man walking around in a brand-new letter sweater?

However, for you ex-athletes out there who've got as fat a belly as I do, this story has a happy ending.

I wouldn't let up. I finally called my mother, who'd been at the game, and she confirmed what I've said. However, what she remembered best, as a mother will, is about me being carried off the field when I got hurt. When I mentioned about the winning touchdown she acted like it was an accomplished fact. She said, "Well of course. Coach Butler came over and told me you won the game for them."

That's a mother for you.

But I wouldn't let it stop there. I wasn't about to let them take away the main truth about my athletic career. The *Banner-Press* notwithstanding, I knew I'd scored that touchdown.

Besides—I've already explained about the exent of our following—the newspaper might not have even had a reporter there that day. After all, Victoria is more than a hundred miles from Brenham. And if it had, he might have been unable to see the players' numbers clearly on account of the field lights and the shadows they caused. Or he might have been out getting a hot dog at just that crucial instant. Anything might have happened.

So I finally called the *Banner-Press* and they were pretty nice about it. Even though it was before his time, Managing Editor Arthur Hahn knew me and knew the story and, though he wouldn't exactly admit that the *Banner-Press* might have made a mistake about the game, he did say he'd *heard* about several mistakes being made on *other* papers. He also said as far as they were concerned, my version was correct. I suggested a present-day front-page correction, nothing beyond reason, just a short five-paragraph box, but he thought, given the time that had passed, that might be excessive.

Which I can understand. But I knew I was the guy who'd scored the touchdown because I was the guy who'd seen the lights sparkling off that football, who'd seen the slow-motion form of the Victoria tacklers and who'd seen, just before getting hit, the broad stripe go under my cleats.

But I still wouldn't let it rest at that. I ran down my old

quarterback, L.M. Killough. And, in a kind of bored voice, he confirmed it.

"Of course," he said, "what's the question here?"

Did you ever notice about quarterbacks? It's always the receivers who go nuts in the end zone. And then the offensive linemen and the backs and the other receivers come running down and jump on the guy.

The quarterback goes over to the sideline and talks with the coach about what looks good on the stock market.

All L.M. said to me about the only touchdown pass I'd ever caught in college football was that he was surprised I hadn't dropped it.

8

Going Down the Road

I think the following piece was a sort of milestone in the publishing history of Sports Illustrated. *Prior to 1979, when I sold them this story, you almost never saw first-person pieces. Oh, certainly there would be the occasional first-person piece by a well-known sports figure, but you never saw a first-hand piece by a semi-nonathlete author who was simply recounting a story that might be of general interest and got by on the basis of its writing quality. Now, since that time, they have short pieces variously called "Insight" and "First Person" and "Sideline," etc.*

It's my belief that "Going Down the Road" was the prototype of their present-day policy. I had originally written the story for Bill Broyles of Texas Monthly *who has since gone on to bigger and better things. But as it turned out he didn't much like the story so he paid me my kill fee and I sent it to* Sports Illustrated *with very little hope. Then, to my great astonishment, my agent called me one morning and said they'd bought it. If I hadn't already been in bed I'd have fainted.*

I was lucky enough to work that little trick quite a few more times than one. I'd get a commission from either Sports Illustrated *or* Texas Monthly, *write the piece, have it turned down, collect my guarantee and then turn around and sell it to the other magazine. Bird's nest on the ground.*

Boy, it was fun while it lasted.

But actually this change in format did have its drawbacks for me. Prior to the acceptance of the first-person style I had primarily written features and what they called "Back of the Book Bonus" pieces. The latter usually could run about 6,000 words and they paid like crazy for them. I had a great editor there at the time, Pat Ryan (more recently the managing editor of Life *magazine), and the farther off the wall the stories were the better Pat liked them. Which was pie for me.*

But with the advent of these shorter pieces, the back-of-the-book-bonus stories went the way of all the lucky breaks free-lance writers get—down the tube.

I guess this story illustrates, better than any other, just how nuts I was about any form of athletics. And, of course, don't confuse a rodeo cowboy with a real cowboy. We were just athletes performing against some very large animals. None of us could have worked cattle or pitched hay or delivered a calf or any of those things that real cowboys do.

Of the people you'll meet in this story, I guess Billy Jack ended up the best. He now owns a janitorial service company in Houston. Jack married his long-time girlfriend and went into farming with her father. Last I heard J.B. was in the hardware business somewhere in South Texas.

I taught Player to fly and he got involved in some of those hare-brained missions that I was doing. He thought, even though I tried to tell him otherwise, that just because an airplane didn't buck it was totally controllable. He died in a crash on a beach in Cuba.

Sometimes I think that the worst thing about making friends is the risk you run of losing them.

The main problem with going rodeoing in the pickup was that there were five of us and nobody wanted to ride in the bed, especially in cold weather.

This was back awhile, back when me and four other worthless cowboys were running the roads all over the Southwest, getting it on down the road from one rodeo to another. I guess it was the pickup that brought us together in the first place. The pickup belonged to Player's daddy, but his daddy would only let him use it ever so often. The rest of us were afoot, which is a damned inconvenient way to go rodeoing. We mostly had to beg or buy rides from other cowboys who might be going to the same rodeo. But we still ended up at a lot of rodeos we didn't want to be at, or riding the bus or hitchhiking. And that was a handicap, given our ability, that none of us needed. It is hard enough to contest the bulls and broncs for a living without throwing in the problem of transportation.

I had known Player from a previous season and it was at a rodeo in Crockett, Texas, that we evolved the idea of hooking up with three or four other cowboys, throwing our luck and gear in together and buying the pickup from Player's dad. I knew J.B., who, as hard as it is to admit, was the best rodeo hand of all of us. He was also an all-round good type and a wonderful fellow. Which is about the worst thing you can say about somebody in rodeo, but in J.B.'s case it wasn't near enough.

And Player knew Jack and Billy Jack and they wanted to come in with us. They both rodeoed about on a par with the rest of us, though Billy Jack was a pretty bad to average bareback rider. They gave us one problem right at the start. They were both named Jack and both wanted to be called that. But of course that wouldn't work, so we cut cards to see which one of them was going to change and the one we called Billy Jack lost. He sulked for a few weeks, wouldn't answer when he was called, but he finally got over it.

Player was about the best man I've ever known, then or since, though he sure didn't look like much. He was a scrawny, dried-up fellow with sandy hair and freckles and had a half-cynical sort of grin on his face all the time. He wasn't even much of a rodeo hand, though he did better in the saddle-bronc than in any of the other events. In spite of that he was just naturally the leader, and it didn't have anything to do with the pickup having been his daddy's. Player was his nickname. He got it from the pitch games we used to have in the clown's trailer before the rodeo. Player seldom lost—in fact, I bet he won more money playing pitch than he did rodeoing—and one time somebody watching said, "Boy, he's a player, ain't he?"

In my own case I was too tall to rodeo the bucking events because I had trouble spurring saddle broncs and bareback horses in the neck. I was a pretty fair bull rider, but I was scared to death of bulls and generally had only half my mind on the ride. The other half was calculating how quick I could get to the fence after I bucked off. Which ain't the best way to ride bulls successfully.

We were all pretty young for that kind of a life. J.B. was the oldest, being 20. I think Player, Jack and Billy Jack were 19. I was 18 and three years too young for my age.

We were rodeoing on the partnership, pooling our expenses and our winnings and splitting them up share and share alike. If, as was often the case, we didn't have the money for everybody to enter all three bucking events, we'd use what we had to get whoever was best in a particular event up in that one and hope to win enough money to make it on down the road to the next rodeo.

We were all RCA cowboys, which meant we either had a Rodeo Cowboys Association card or a permit. The RCA (it's now the PRCA, the P standing for Professional) was the governing organization for professional rodeo, though at its best it was still a pretty loose operation. But the RCA sponsored all the big shows, the rodeos with added money that put up the best purses. Being members of the RCA, we could compete in these shows. The drawback was that we couldn't legally compete in those little independent rodeos generally held in small towns over some holiday like Labor Day or the Fourth of July. If the RCA caught you in those local shows, they'd either fine you or suspend you for a time. What was worse was getting caught by the local cowboys if you entered one. Not being RCA cowboys they could only compete around home, and they resented us professionals coming in and trying to win their local money. What they'd do, if they caught you, was beat the hell out of you and everybody with you.

But the problem for us was that we weren't good enough to compete and win money at the big rodeos. Our style was to find out where the good cowboys were heading and go the other way. We were still a good deal better than the locals, and working the little rodeos was an important source of income. Naturally we got caught fairly often. It was one of these situations, when Jack and Billy Jack got the hell beat out of them, that caused us to invent the double-barreled pickup and resulted in us stealing a bench out of the bus station in Amarillo, Texas.

What happened was that Billy Jack got recognized by another cowboy as being RCA at a little rodeo in Hull Daisetta. Jack had the misfortune to be with Billy Jack at the time, and about eight of those old country boys got the two of them behind the chute and commenced to throb their knobs. Me and Player had taken a count and decided there was no point in us getting mixed up in it. Se we had got ourselves good seats on the fence where we could see the fight, what there was of it. J.B., being the wonderful human being he was, had gone and sat in the pickup. I didn't blame him for not getting in the fight, but I did think he could at least have had the decency to watch. But that was J.B., never a thought for his friends.

When we finally got away that night there was a cold wind

blowing. Jack and Billy Jack were riding in the bed, where we'd put them after the locals had got through with them. After they came to and all the way until our first stop they were hollering and banging on the rear window, which made it hard for us in the cab to hear the radio. Then when we stopped for gas they went to whining and moaning about the cold wind. They were considerably lacerated about the head and face and they complained that the wind made their cuts burn even worse. It didn't sound like that big a deal to me and Player, but the upshot was they insisted on riding in the cab, and riding five in a pickup cab, especially if the other four are unwashed and smelly, ain't any bed of roses.

Well, we decided we had to do something. We'd had trouble the whole time about who was going to ride in the bed and who in the cab. At first we'd decided the fair thing was for the three high money winners at each rodeo to ride in the cab, but that hadn't worked. There were times when nobody won anything and other times when there'd be four tied for second place with a grand total of zero. That kind of a situation brought on nothing but squabbles, a commodity we were already overstocked on.

So there was nothing for it but to make some changes. Right after the next rodeo we left the circuit and went to Temple, where Player's parents lived, and got hold of a cutting torch and cut the rear third out of the cab and moved it back about three feet. Then we took some sheet metal and welded it in the open space and ended up with a long cab body big enough for two seats. Of course they have that kind of pickup now, but our innovation may have been the first of its kind. We called it a double-barreled pickup, and it was probably the ugliest vehicle I've ever seen on the road. Naturally we didn't bother to paint the sheet iron we'd patched it with. We were in too big a hurry to get back to rodeoing, so as soon as we'd made it weathertight we threw our rigging bags in the bed and took off.

All the other hands on the circuit thought the double-barreled pickup was about the funniest thing they'd ever seen. We'd come skidding up to an arena, running late as usual, and everybody around the chutes would start laughing. But the pickup ran good. It was only about five or six years old at the time and very dependable. I think it would have gotten good gas mileage if we hadn't forever been driving 85 and 90 miles an hour. We'd bought it from Player's daddy for $900 and we sent him a money order every week for $25 from wherever we were. We were pretty determined about keeping up those payments, and more than once we shorted ourselves on grub to get that money in. I guess we were that way because Player's daddy was a fine man and we didn't want him to find out just what a bunch of worthless no-goods his son was running with.

Once, at a rodeo in Brownwood, we were really down on it. We'd spent our last cent to get to the show and hadn't a one of us won a nickel by the time we got to the bull riding, which is the last event. J.B. and Billy Jack and me were all in the bulls, but both of them had already bucked off, which left it up to me.

You'd of thought it was the World Series the way those other four gathered around my chute and began having a prayer meeting with my heart. They were giving me more help getting down on that bull than I could just about stand. Of course, they all knew I was scared of bulls. You don't hide something like that in rodeo.

They were all up on the boards behind the chute. Jack and Billy Jack were helping me get down, J.B. was saying, "Shoot, this ain't no bull. Anybody could ride this animal." Player was quietly pulling my bull rope and giving me advice about how much rope to take. You ride a bull with what they call a bull rope that goes around his middle with a bell on the bottom. You never actually tie it off, but rather take several wraps around your hand in such a fashion that when you buck off it comes loose and you won't get hung up and get your arm yanked out of the socket.

But of course that happens anyway.

You tighten your bull rope around the bull's chest depending on how strong you think he is. A bull's muscles swell an uncommon amount when he explodes out of the chute and he'll snap that rope right away from you if you take too tight a pull.

I'd got down on him, feeling all that power between my legs, looking at his ears, which were about the size of quart bottles, worrying that I was going to get killed. He'd throw his head back every once in a while, giving me a malicious look and slinging strings of slobber at me. I'd already been told about this bull. He was bad to ride and bad to fight. He was a spinning bull, which meant he'd come out of the chute, turn back to the left, and go into a tight spin. Most non-rodeo people don't know that bucking stock will do just about the same thing every time they come out of the chute. For this reason you can generally go around and ask about the particular animal you've drawn and there is sure to be some cowboy who's had him before and knows what he'll do.

This particular bull was a money bull. On a ride, half the score is based on what the contestant does, the other half on how well the animal bucks, and this one I'd drawn was a good one. If I could put a ride on him I'd be sure to place in the money. For that matter, I didn't have to make much of a ride. This rodeo featured a particularly good string of bucking bulls, and just about all I had to do was hang on for eight seconds and we'd make some cash.

But I was scared. "This bull is bad to fight!" I said.

J.B. said, "Huh! He don't scare me."

And Player said, "Naw, he ain't. Don't even think about that. This is a gentle bull. Like a rocking chair."

"Don't tell me that! I've asked six cowboys and all six say he is bad to fight."

"Now, listen," Player said, "we are flat broke and the payment on the pickup is due. If you don't put a ride on this bull we're going to have to call Raymond (he called his daddy Raymond) and tell him we can't make the payment. And we're going up there in a week for Thanksgiving. How'll you feel about that?"

Then the stock contractor was there, tapping the chute gate with his hotshot and asking me if I was ready. I cocked my toes up to get my spurs lower so I could get them under the barrel of the bull, tugged my hat tighter, tensed up, and said, "Outside." The chute gate opened and that bull exploded and, oh, was he strong. Sure enough, he took about two jumps into the arena, cut back and started spinning. He would have lost me if I hadn't been prepared for that cutback. As it was, he nearly got me when he started into his spin. The way you ride a spinning bull is to really get down and deep with the spur that's to the inside of the spin. If you lose that one you're gone. You don't ride a bull with the strength of your arm. Nobody's that strong. You ride him with your spurs and with balance.

I didn't remember much about the spin. About halfway through I sort of blacked out. When I came to I was about half off his side on the inside of the spin, just barely hanging on. The buzzer sounded at about the time my hand gave out and I went tumbling in the dust. As it turned out, two bulls got ridden that night and mine was one of them. I got second money, which allowed us to pay the pickup note and get on down the road to the next rodeo.

We didn't solve our seating problem with the double-barreled pickup straight off. True, we'd created three feet more space behind the front seat, but the accommodations didn't suit the parties involved. We had first tried putting two camp stools back there, but what with the way we drove, the people sitting on them were constantly being upset and thrown around until they got pretty badly bruised up. Billy Jack complained that he was getting hurt worse going to the rodeo than he was in it.

Well, we knew we had to do something, but we didn't know what. A regular back seat out of a car wouldn't fit there, nor would the two lawn chairs that we'd borrowed out of a front yard in San Saba. If the mother of invention is necessity, then I suppose it was that mother that caused us to steal the bench out of the Greyhound bus station in Amarillo.

We didn't go to Amarillo to deliberately steal a bench. We had gone there for an RCA rodeo, a happenstance that came about because we couldn't find any independent rodeos to poach on. Naturally we didn't win a cent. But a Texas beer company was putting on a rodeo promotion and they had free beer and hot dogs for all the contestants after the show. That solved the problem of supper and the night's entertainment.

But it was good and late when we pulled away from the rodeo arena heading for Breckenridge. We had to go through town on the way out. Jack and Billy Jack were in the back on the camp stools, having a good deal more trouble staying mounted than usual because of the cargo of beer they'd taken on. Player was driving and J.B. was sitting in the middle acting like he was one of the grown-ups. We stopped at a light and I happened to glance over at the bus station, which was on the corner. I could see right into the lobby and in that instant the mother of invention raised her head. I told Player to back up to the curb.

"What for?" he asked me.

"I got an idea," I said. "Just do it."

We parked and I outlined what I had in mind. Everybody turned around and craned their necks to see into the lobby. It was deserted. We could make out a ticket agent and a real ugly girl behind the lunch counter and what appeared to be an old, old Indian sitting against a far wall.

Player was enthusiastic about the idea, Jack and Billy Jack less so because it was taking them so long to understand what we were going to do. J.B. just folded his arms and flatly declared he'd have nothing to do with it. He said, "I ain't stealing no property from the Greyhound Bus Company. You never heard of them interstate laws? It's a Federal offense is what it is. I would just as soon steal from the Mrs. Baird's Bread Company."

But we didn't need him anyway. We explained to Jack and Billy Jack what they were supposed to do and then Player and I went on into the bus station. It was as deserted as it had looked from outside, just the ticket agent, the girl, and the old Indian against the wall. Player headed for the ticket agent and I went to the lunch counter. Our objective was to maintain as much eye contact with our targets as we could in order to keep them from noticing what was happening with one of the bus company's benches. Player handled the ticket agent by asking him for a route to some unorthodox place like Glendive, Montana, and I concentrated on this remarkably ugly girl. She had pimples and thick glasses and an overbite, but I went up and sat down on a stool and ordered a cup of coffee and told her I thought I was in love.

Meanwhile, behind us Billy Jack and Jack had come in and each had taken an end of the bench and they were busy carrying it out the door. Out of the corner of my eye I could follow their progress by the old Indian. As they went toward the door his head slowly turned to follow them, his face expressionless. When they were clear he returned his head to its original position and resumed staring into space.

Player then told the ticket agent he'd changed his mind, that he was going to bed instead of Glendive, and I told the girl I'd just remembered I was married and we got the hell out of there.

The bench was just a fit. It was one of those lightweight chrome and leatherette jobs rigged out to handle two people. It slid in behind the front seat like it was designed for the job. We went to Breckenridge and stopped off there at a little welding shop and for a dollar we had the legs spot-welded to the floor. After that we were rigged out as well as anyone could want.

Not that it helped our rodeoing any. We finished out the season about as bad as we'd started.

I don't know why any of us rodeoed. Certainly it wasn't the money. We could have made more clerking part-time in a grocery store. And it wasn't the fame or the glamour, because none of us ever ran up on such a thing. That was for a very few stars who actually knew what they were doing when they got down on a head of bucking stock.

But there were compensations. One of the most attractive was the Shiny Brights. Shiny Brights were especially good-looking girls who hung around the rodeos and who liked tight jeans and rodeo cowboys. That was one of the few elements that gave the life an occasional pleasant quality. To make it with the Shiny Brights you didn't have to be smart or rich or good-looking. About all you had to do was say, "I drawed me a good bronc in the second go-round and I might be sitting tall for day money."

That kind of talk. Worked every time.

But, all in all, it wasn't a comfortable life. We didn't eat in many restaurants. Mostly we bought our food in grocery stores, making out with Vienna sausage and bologna and crackers and cheese and apples. It wasn't the best diet, but we were all young and strong and I doubt if the bubonic plague would have slowed us down much.

We had about the same situation on accommodations. We'd find the cheapest motel we could and one of us would go in and rent a single. Then about an hour later the rest of us would come slipping in. At night we'd take the mattress off the box spring and three of us would sleep crosswise on the mattress and two crosswise on the box springs. Or we did until I got a sleeping bag. After that I found me a quiet corner and slept on the floor.

Naturally we were always getting discovered and thrown out. And if the management wasn't smart enough to figure out what we were doing, J.B. would sometimes help them. Once we were in this motel in Wichita Falls, four of us in there without paying, and J.B. went down to the office and complained to the clerk that there weren't enough towels.

In the final analysis, I guess we were rodeo cowboys because we liked the feeling. Maybe it was nothing more than the fact that we could wear big hats and put our pants legs in our boots if we wanted to and nobody was going to mistake us for Rexall Rangers.

Still, it was a dangerous life. You got hurt a little bit every time you came out of the chutes, even if you didn't get in what we called a wreck. Riding bucking bareback horses may be the worst for a sustained type of injury. In that event, your rigging is a wide leather band that cinches upon the horse's chest with a thing a little like a suitcase handle to hang onto with one hand. The problem is the position you have to assume to make a successful ride. Just as you call for the gate, you tense your riding arm and lean almost all the way back on the horse, bringing your legs up so you can mark him in the shoulders as you pass the judges. The position you're in, you tend to go backward when he surges out of the gate and forward when the horse sucks back on you, which they are very prone to do. This tends to tear up the elbow in your riding arm as well as the hand itself. And the spurring is rough on the knees. If you'll notice carefully at your next rodeo, you'll note that most contestants in the bareback event wear some sort of support on either one or both knees.

Of course, bulls are the ultimate danger. They are so big and strong that they can just brush up against you and send you tumbling. The horns of rodeo bulls are blunt, but that doesn't make much difference. If they get a solid shot at your chest they're going to break ribs, and a broken rib through the lungs is not much different from a goring. It's very easy to tell when it's time for the bull-riding event, even without benefit of the announcer. If you listen closely you'll discover how quiet it gets behind the chute. You'll also hear an occasional prayer.

When we went rodeoing the next season, things weren't quite the same. J.B., that wonderful human being, was starting to win consistently and that put a certain strain on the relationship all around. Since we were still splitting expenses and winnings, J.B. developed the habit, after a couple of rodeos in which he'd done better than the rest of us, of saying, ominously, "I ain't naming no names, but they's a few sonofabitches riding in this pickup ain't carrying their share of the load."

Even Billy Jack developed a style of saddle-bronc riding that was moving him a class ahead of the rest of us. That pretty well broke up the partnership. We'd got the pickup paid for, so Player borrowed some money from Raymond and bought the other three out. Me and Player tried it a while longer, but we found ourselves splitting zero a little too often to make traveling expenses. Finally we just kind of slid off on our own.

As for the double-barreled pickup, the last I heard, it had quit rodeoing also and gone on to hauling hay back on Raymond's farm.

9

A Season with the Press Club Spikes

This whole mess, an episode that I'm not too proud of, started innocently enough at a Press Club picnic that a beer distributor in Houston threw for us. We had a pickup softball game that I pitched and hit several home runs in and thought no more about.

Until about a week later a guy named Sam Caldwell, who is a commercial artist in Houston, came up to me and said let's get up a softball team and enter a league. Well, I just laughed at him. I told him I was a baseball player and that I didn't play mush *ball. But he persisted.*

Everything that happened after that was Sam's fault.

I have had a mortifying sin ulcerating on my soul since 1969, and I believe the time has come to clean the bases, so to speak, and to deglorify the only athletic trophy in the Press Club in Houston.

I refer to the time that the Press Club Spikes won the Commercial Division of the Fast Pitch League of Greater Houston. It all began innocently enough when the entire Press Club was invited to a picnic at the ranch of Frank Horlock, a local beer distributor. We played your average picnic softball game. Now I'm not trying to puff myself up, but I had played semi-pro ball and I even had a tryout with the St. Louis Cardinals, so I was a slight cut above the other members of the Press Club. I hit a couple of home runs and pitched, striking out the side a few times, and my team won by about 16 runs.

I thought no more about it, other than its having been a good time, until about a week later. I was sitting in the Press Club, quietly sipping a lemonade when Sam Caldwell came in. Sam had been the organizer of the softball game.

Sam is an extremely fine illustrator, but the fire of a competitive athlete burns in his nonathletic body. He walked over and sat down in a chair at my table and said, "Well, I've entered us in the league."

I said, mildly, "What league?" thinking he meant the Art League or something like that.

But Sam said, "Commercial Division, fast pitch."

I just looked at him, not quite certain what I was hearing. I said, "You've entered who?"

He said, "The Press Club Spikes. Like the name?"

Lemonade wasn't strong enough for what I was hearing. So I turned around to the bartender and signaled him to bring me a cola.

Sam said, "I know you're a good hitter and a pretty good chunker so I figure we have a chance. I talked to the board and they agreed to put up the entry fee, so I went ahead and entered us."

I almost choked. I said, "Sam, you ain't including me in this, are you? I mean, not based on that pickup game? I was pitching and hitting against forty-year-old nonathletes and twelve-year-old girls."

But Sam was getting up. He said, "Hell, you can do it."

I said, "Sit down, Sam! Do what?"

Sam said, "Why, you're the manager and the pitcher."

I leaned forward and said, "In the Commercial Division? Fast pitch? Have you lost what little is left of your mind? You're talking Xerox, Conoco, IBM, Phillips Petroleum. They've got thousands of employees to pick from, many of whom have been athletes. We're talking about the Press Club *members*, half of whom are women. With me as the pitcher? I can't throw the ball underhand much more than twenty miles an hour. I'm an infielder! A good team will have a windmiller who can bring it up there at seventy miles an hour and make it rise or sink or curve. Get serious!"

Sam just put both his hands on his knees and said, "We've got to do it. I've already ordered caps for the team."

Then he got up and left.

Caps?

Most of these teams were dressed by the same companies who

provided uniforms for major league clubs. I had tried out a couple of years before for one of these teams and didn't make it. Now I was to play and manage against them? And Sam's talking to me about caps?

I slumped back in my chair and hoped the elevators wouldn't work so I would never be able to get out of that place and face what I knew was coming.

I vividly remember the cold, windy March day I held the tryout for the actual members of the Press Club (Sam had put a notice on the bulletin board in *Gothic* lettering). I'm not saying they were bad, but I had some "players" out there who didn't know if they needed a left-handed or right-handed glove because they didn't know which arm they threw with. The sportswriters were the worst. I am convinced, though I have no documentation, that within every sportswriter lurks a frustrated athlete. Well, these guys were simply frustrating.

Watching them, I understood what Casey Stengel, managing the Mets in their first season, meant when he said of his outfield, "I got two guys out there who can't play, and the other one can't catch the ball."

I stuck with an old baseball axiom and looked for strength up the middle. So I kept trying guys at second base to see if they could take a throw with a runner barreling in on them from first base. I was the runner. Most times there was no point in sliding high because the ball had either already sailed into center field or the second baseman had dropped it by the time I got there. But, finally, one feisty little guy from the entertainment section of the *Chronicle* had the ball waiting for me. I hit him in the chest, and he went one way and the ball went the other. I got up and was dusting myself off when he came at me, flailing his arms and saying words I wouldn't want your children to hear. I didn't pay much attention to it, but, when I got back over to the sidelines, Sam said, "Why didn't you hit him back?"

"Hit him back?" I said. "Why, did he hit me?"

That convinced me. I could picture both benches emptying during a brawl. I would be getting the living daylights beat out of me while my guys would be out there interviewing the other team as to just how many and what kind of punches they had hit me with.

For the sake of form, we played a couple of practice games

against church-league teams (about four notches below the Commercial level), and they beat us so bad the ten-run rule went into effect in the second inning in both games.

After that, I had a quiet talk with Horlock, whose company was furnishing us with uniforms and equipment and handling the other expenses. Horlock agreed with my plan, and the next day new faces started showing up at our practices.

I brought in Phil Gray, a former college track star, as my catcher. I brought in Billy Paul as my right fielder and clean-up hitter; he had played at Texas A & M. I brought in Jim Hughey, who had played at Texas. My pitcher was an unlikely find, in the form of a preacher from a small church outside of Houston. I don't know how he performed in the pulpit, but he could make that softball do everything but take up the collection. For my reliever and starter against the weaker teams (when the reverend was otherwise occupied with good works), I tapped no less than the Texas legislature for Russell Cummings, a very cute rocker-armer.

But my big find was Larry Prevatt, a cat-quick shortstop who could hit and run and field with anyone. How he had been overlooked by the Major City League, I could never imagine.

By the time I had finished recruiting and had filed my roster with the City Parks and Recreation Department, I was the only member of the starting team who was an actual member of the Press Club. Of course, I kept some Press Club members in uniform, fully intending to let them play if we ever got way ahead or hopelessly behind. But you know fast-pitch softball. Most games are one- or two-run affairs. So they didn't get in there very often. I still feel kind of bad about that, but as Walter Matthau said to Tatum O'Neal, "That's baseball."

Still, they made their contributions. We had the best cheering section in the league. And one sportswriter, who I know ached to get into the game, was a genius at charting the other teams' tendencies against our starting pitcher. Sam even sketched a series of cartoons illustrating our signs. I never did get around to telling him that we changed them every game. It was a good bench. In fact, the only problem I had with them, ringers and nonringers alike, was keeping their language cleaned up around the preacher.

Of course, I'm not going to tell you what the ringers got paid. Let's just say they got more "gas money" than anyone else, as well as an almost unlimited supply of Horlock's product.

Well, the season rocked along, and it quickly became obvious it was between us and Xerox. We were in first place going into our final game with Conoco, but we lost it on a throwing error by our playing manager/third baseman. That led to a playoff with Xerox.

It figured to be a tight one because we played hit and run. By that I mean a hit batsman, take your base, steal second, steal third, and come in on anything. Prevatt had standing orders to run anytime he could. Gray had been an intercollegiate broad jumper, and he could sprint. My second baseman could run and I had once run a pretty good hundred in college. So our game plan was to turn a walk, or anything, into a triple.

But Xerox had a new face at shortstop, a guy we had never seen before. He was listed on the lineup card as George West. We had always been able to steal on their catcher, but we couldn't steal on George. It didn't matter if the ball was high or wide, he would catch it, do a flip in the air, and tag you out. And if the throw was on the money, you were not going to dislodge George, no matter how hard you slid.

So they took our entire game away from us. And forget about getting the ball to the left side. George would cut in front of the third baseman, do a pirouette, and throw you out.

I'm talking swift and strong. The final score was 2–1, in Xerox's favor. George scored both of their runs. Prevatt hit an inside-the-park home run for our only score. But it was I who won the championship and claimed the trophy that still resides inside a glass case at the Houston Press Club. And I did it without getting a hit.

The next day I went down to the League office and filed a protest that Xerox had run in a ringer on us in order to win the championship. The director looked over their roster, which had been filed at the beginning of the season, and George West was not listed. My protest was upheld, and we were declared the winner.

That sound pretty chicken, doesn't it? And my soul still burns about what I did. But in my defense, I already knew that George was a "loaner" from a Major City League team, and I ask you to judge me with that in mind.

The next day the manager of the Xerox club called and asked me to meet him for coffee. We sat there in the restaurant of a Holiday Inn, not saying much until he finally blurted out, "How could you do that? File that protest? You hypocrite, you had a field full of ringers. Hell, half your team couldn't read, much less write! Explain that!"

I said, "Because your ringer was so much better than mine."

It took him so off-guard he just sat there for a minute, fiddling with his cup. Then he sighed and got up. "I guess you're right," he said. "No hard feelings. At the beginning of the season we had a good laugh about playing the Press Club. I just didn't know you'd have enough gall to call my hand."

I rest my case. And maybe my soul.

10

The Joy of Six

*In about 1970, give or take a year, Bill Broyles pulled up in my driveway in Houston and said he was the editor of a new magazine (*Texas Monthly*) and asked would I write for them. Naturally I asked him what he paid. The figure he named was about a tenth of what I was getting for the pieces I was doing for national magazines.*

So I just kind of started laughing. But Bill persisted. Now Bill is likeable. I don't know anyone who doesn't like Bill Broyles. I finally asked him if he had any beer money and he said he did so we went out and had a few.

Not quite correct. I had a few. Bill nursed one all through the course of the evening. Most writers drink; editors don't. That's because editors have that blue pencil which is their greatest sedative.

But by the time we got back to my house I'd agreed to write for Bill.

Now it's some years later and I want to do this piece on six-man football. I call Bill and he says he's never heard of six-man football. Of course I knew he'd been president of the student body at Rice University and I knew he'd been a Fulbright scholar at Oxford, but I didn't think he'd gotten that far away from his roots.

So I didn't try to argue with him. I just said, "Bill, you remember when you got me to work for you for $250 a story?"

There was a pause and then he said, "How about a $1 thousand guarantee against a $2 thousand fee? And all expenses of course."

The funny thing was that Bill and the whole staff at Texas Monthly *got hooked on the fortunes of the Cherokee team. The story I wrote was early in the season. Every week, until Cherokee lost, Bill and the staff followed them like Ivan Boesky used to follow the stock market.*

He told me once that he considered this one of the best stories I ever did for him. That's when I found out that editors are fallible. They'd had me convinced to the contrary up to that point.

R oddy Maddox was nervous, fidgeting and walking back and forth as he waited for the school pep rally to begin. He kept complaining about his back, claiming he had hurt it a few days before while slinging feed to his pigs and moving fence posts. Someone suggested to the coach that his injury might be psychosomatic, and Maddox looked outraged. "Why, it is not! Nerves haven't got a thing to do with it. My back hurts, that's all."

Maddox is head coach of the Cherokee Indians. The game his team would be playing that night, and the game that was making his back hurt, was six-man football.

"Shoot, there's a lot of people never even heard of six-man football," Maddox said. "And a lot of them who have don't think anybody plays it anymore. Well, there's fifty-five high schools in Texas that do, and for us here in Cherokee it's the *only* kind of football, and we get just as excited about every game as any team in the country."

He stood outside the dressing room, staring at the field. "Boy, we got to have this one." He spit tobacco juice. "I mean we really got to have it."

"I believe we're ready, coach," said assistant coach James Low.

"You can't ever be *too* ready," Maddox said nervously. "Not for a game like this."

Six-man football was devised for schools with small enrollments. It was first played in the thirties in Nebraska, and the Texas University Interscholastic League adopted it in 1938. Nationwide, six-man has become a sports oddity, but it still thrives in Texas (Colorado is the only other state playing the game and it has only three teams). Cherokee, which is eighteen miles north of Llano on the road to Fort Worth, has a population of two hundred and it fulfills the UIL's one absolute rule about six-man football: Cherokee High School has fewer than 75 students. To be exact, it has 21 boys and 11 girls. Of the 21 boys, 20 are involved in the football program, 19 playing and one acting as manager. The twenty-first would like to play, but his parents won't let him.

All the girls are on the pep squad.

Cherokee had already played two non-district games, shutting out Oglesby 39–0 and losing to Paint Rock, 44–34. The game this night was the first district game, which made it special enough, but what made it more so was their opponent, Richland Springs. Richland Springs, 32 miles away, is about twice the size of Cherokee. There is a natural rivalry between the two towns, but it was now coming to a head with their first football game. Until the previous year, when its enrollment had dropped, Richland Springs had played eleven-man football, and the Richland players were reportedly contemptuous of what they considered a lesser game.

Troy Boultinghouse, who plays end for the Indians, said, "We'd seen them over at the movies in San Saba or at the cafe, and they acted like there was nothing to six-man, that they were just going to throb our knobs and show us what the game was all about. Well, they're going to get their chance tonight."

In six-man football three players are in the line and three in the backfield. Because of the shortage of personnel and the wide-open style of play, every player usually learns more than one position, and you will frequently see running backs rotating to ends and even centers becoming quarterbacks. This is a circumstance that could hardly be imagined in the specialized game of eleven-man, but in six-man the players seem to thrive on the diversity. Everyone on the team, including the center, is an eligible pass receiver. However, the quarterback cannot advance the ball across the line of scrimmage on a run unless he has first handed the ball off or passed it and then received it back. The team can line up in every conceivable formation, from the straight T, to a spread, to the I, punt, shotgun, or any number of variations.

There are several other ways six-man differs from eleven-man. First, the field is only eighty yards long and forty yards wide (a regular field is a hundred yards by 160 feet). Players do not go ten yards for a first down but fifteen. The goal posts are different, too. On a regular goal the cross bar is 10 feet high, the side posts 23 feet apart. In six-man the dimensions are 9 and 25 feet.

The score for the extra point is exactly reversed from eleven-man (a kick counts two points, a run or pass one) because it is easier to pass or run for the three yards than it is to kick.

There is also a scoring limitation. If either team gets 45 points ahead by halftime, or during the second half, the game is over. This makes for some maverick plays when the winning team, simply for the fun of it, wants to finish the game by the clock. You are likely to see missed snaps and fumbles and intercepted passes and missed tackles until the losing team catches up enough so that the superior team can put its offense back to work.

What it comes down to is a wild, exciting, high-scoring game. With fewer players on the field you can see more of the action, watch the plays developing, and easily single out the performance of individual players. Every play is designed to score from anywhere on the field, so there are more gadget plays, more sweeps and reverses, and fewer of the straight-ahead lunges so prevalent in eleven-man.

Maddox at thirty-six still has the look of a running back. He has gotten his teams into the state championship playoffs three times. Twice they won and the third time they lost by only two points. Cherokee, like most six-man football high schools, has no football budget, so getting into the playoffs would mean three extra games, worth as much as $2,000 in revenue.

"I just hope we can give Richland a game," Maddox said. "But I would sure hate to lose this first one. Any of them, for that matter, because you've about got to go undefeated to get into the playoffs for state, and if we don't make state we have a hard time raising money for the program, even with the help of the booster club."

In the afternoon Maddox sent his players home with the strong admonition to get off their feet and get some rest. "I don't want no running up and down the roads in your cars, you hear? You rest and think about this game."

They said, "Yessir," which is the way his players talk to Maddox, and to everyone else for that matter. As football players go, they are not big. The biggest is Robbie Broyles at 185 pounds. The running back, Jim McDoniel, weighs 180. After that the size falls off rapidly. At a large AAAA school there might be seven hundred or eight hundred boys, and obviously many of them will be above average in weight and height. Out of twenty-one boys, Maddox felt lucky to have what size he did.

But now it was getting closer to game time, and a few members of the booster club came out to start their fires in the barbecue pits at the end of the field. They would cook hamburgers for the pep rally and serve them in the school cafeteria at $2 a plate.

The informal, unofficial booster club in Cherokee holds regular morning meetings at Boultinghouse's Texaco service station, standing around, matching for drinks, and arguing about the upcoming game. All the men in Cherokee are unofficial members and many of the wives help out at the concession stands or with the pep squad.

"We couldn't make it without them," Maddox said. "We don't ever have no fund-raisings as such, but if we need something, all we do is tell someone and first thing you know he's back saying, `Well, we got the money for that. Now what else can we help with?' They just go around, and this one will give ten dollars and that one twenty, and the next thing you know there's the money."

He stood in the tiny visitors' dressing room, pointing at a weight machine. "They bought us that Universal gym set. And they put the chain-link fence around the field. Put that big billboard up outside of town that says we're state champions."

Outside it was misting slightly. It had been raining off and on all day, and parts of the ground around the small bleachers and the concession stand were muddy. Herman Rhoades and John Ed Keeney had shown up earlier in the afternoon with fifteen yards of crushed gravel and were spreading it over the worst areas.

Someone wondered who asked them to do that. Maddox shook his head. "Nobody. They just seen it needed doing, so they went over to the county barn and borrowed a truck and done it."

Maddox wasn't getting any calmer. "I hope this rain lets up," he said, looking up at the sky, "because I'm afraid we're liable to have to pass on those big old Richland boys—for what little chance that will give us."

Wilson Kuykendall, working at the barbecue pits, ventured the opinion that Cherokee would win 56 to 20.

Maddox said, "Oh, don't start that old stuff. I don't want to hear it. Good heavens!"

And then someone asked Lawton Yarborough how his son Larry, who is the quarterback, was doing. Larry had hurt his passing arm in a scrimmage the past week. "Pretty good, I guess," he answered. "Course it would be doing a lot better, but he got in an acorn chunkin' fight with his little brother just as I was leaving the house and reinjured it."

"Oh, lordy," Maddox said, "I'm leaving. I got work."

He got in his pickup and drove out to where he keeps a number of hogs and pigs and fed them. After that he went into town, picked up a load of groceries and took them out to José Soto, the hired man who runs his small turkey operation. "We got to have this one," he said to the man, "I mean we really got to have it."

"*Sí*," said José, who doesn't speak any English.

"Now, you be pulling for us, hear?"

"*Sí*," José said.

Maddox spent a few minutes looking over the flock of about three thousand laying turkeys, then got in his truck and headed for his house.

Turkey farming is the principal industry in Cherokee. Without it the town probably couldn't exist. The countryside may be nice to look at, but the ground is hard and rocky and prevents farming and discourages cattle raising on any scale. Only the hunters who take deer leases add anything to the economy. Cherokee seems prosperous, perhaps because the inhabitants will it so. Apparently few people ever leave and those who do by all accounts would like to come back.

W.O. Boultinghouse, a large, bulky man in bib overalls who runs the Texaco station, where the booster club meets, said, "I was up in Austin for a time, but I was looking back here the whole spell. I guess if there were homes and jobs enough for everybody that ever left, 90 percent of them would be back here before kickoff tonight."

The rain had stopped and the weather had turned crisp with the solid taste of fall that goes with football. In the school cafeteria they were doing a rush-order business on the hamburgers and potato salad and beans. On top of everything else it was homecoming and there were even three representatives from the class of 1928.

Some of the players started wandering into the field house, those who had special taping to do or who were just too nervous to stay at home. Richland Springs arrived at 6:30, and Maddox went out to meet their coach, Ralph Bates. "Just hope we can give you a game," Bates said.

The Cherokee players dressed, some of them going outside the tiny field house dressing room to finish up because there wasn't enough room inside. It was getting close to time and the tension was showing.

"Getting their game faces on," Maddox said nervously. He'd had his on all day. He went over to confer with James Low one last time about the plays they planned to concentrate on, reading off a little pad he held in his hand, palming it like a card shark.

The stands were starting to fill up. Astonishingly so. People were even beginning to line up along the chain-link fence surrounding the field. There were already more spectators at the game than the population of the whole town.

John Altizer, who owns the best coon dog in the county, named Old Nasty, said, "Oh, they come from all around to our games. Once you've seen six-man football, it kind of spoils you for anything else. In six-man you can see everything. It's wide open, not that three yards and a cloud of dust stuff."

The air of anticipation in the stands and on the field was substantial. The players on the field looked dim under the sparsely placed arc lights, but the Richland boys did indeed look bigger than the Cherokee Indians. Over on the sideline Maddox jiggled and fidgeted as the kickoff sailed high through the air.

"C'mon, c'mon!" he yelled, as his team surged down the field to cover the kickoff.

Richland lined up in an awkward-looking spread formation, ineffective because it required more ball handling and took more time for a play to develop. They tried a run that didn't work and then tried a pass, which Larry Yarborough intercepted and returned thirty yards for a touchdown.

It wasn't very close. Richland couldn't move on their next possession, and Cherokee took over, immediately scoring a twenty-yard run by Edward Jones. Richland seemed confused by the swiftness and precision of the Cherokee attack. From a tight formation one of the Indians' little backs would suddenly come bursting up the middle, or go wide on a sweep, or slash off tackle on a twisting, darting run. When they had the ball Richland would try plays from their clumsy wide formation and would suddenly find their backfield full of hard-tackling Indians who stopped them before they could get started.

By the half the score was 37 to 7, and Maddox had already begun substituting his second-string players. The only Richland score had come on a kickoff return when one of the second-stringers had let the return man get outside him.

In the second half Cherokee got into trouble. They had scored two touchdowns, one on a 27-yard run by Mike Briseno, and the score had shot up to 51 to 7. If they kicked the extra point they would lead by more than 45 points and the game would be over. Maddox and Low, who double as math teachers, were staring up at the scoreboard, mentally adding and subtracting, trying to figure out the difference. Next morning at the regular booster club meeting at the service station, Glen Jones would say, "That was one of the funniest things I've ever seen. Them two math teachers down their countin' on their fingers, tryin' to see how far they were ahead."

To keep from stopping the game, Maddox sent in a freshman, Wyman Jones, who had never kicked anything but a can, to try the extra point. But that wasn't enough guarantee for the team. Wyman just might get lucky, so they arranged for the center to snap the ball along the ground, making sure they'd get to play the rest of the game.

It ended 57 to 14 and Maddox finally looked calm. Then someone reminded him how easy it had been. "Oh, no," he said, "don't say that. We got May next week and I'm not even sure if we can give them a game."

There was a good turnout for the booster club the next morning. One of the members, a bottle of Delaware Punch in hand, said, "Well, I hope we done our duty by givin' that bunch from Richland Springs a lesson in six-man football."

"I think they got the message," House said.

Standing outside his third-period math class, Roddy Maddox said, "I hope we don't ever get so big that we've got to go on to eleven-man. I like this six-man football. It gives me more time to work with each individual boy, and it gives him a chance to feel he's important and making a real contribution to the team. I don't ever want to coach anywhere else. If they offered me the head job at the biggest school in Houston, I wouldn't take it."

Maddox thinks there will always be six-man football. "I don't see why not. There's always going to be enough little towns like Cherokee that will keep the game going. Shoot, if we can make it here in Cherokee on turkeys, other folks can make it wherever they are with whatever they got. This game will keep going."

Since the end of the game Maddox hadn't said a word about his back hurting. It probably wouldn't flare up again until the day of the game with May.

Cherokee later defeated Cotton Center to win the state six-man football championship.

11

Putting Up with a Lot of Bull

Through the years I had constantly pressed Sports Illustrated *to let me do more rodeo pieces because I knew rodeo about as well as anybody did and, consequently, the stories were easier for me. I'd even written the research piece for the* Encyclopedia Americana *and I had a lot of friends in the sport.*

But my editors stayed lukewarm, claiming that rodeo wasn't of especially wide appeal.

Then my editor of preference, Linda Verigan, was taken to a rodeo at Madison Square Garden and got all excited and called me the next morning and asked if I'd ever heard of a rodeo clown named Leon Coffee.

Since I'd only known Leon about eight or nine years and was still smarting from their New York attitude toward rodeo I'd said, no, but tell me about him.

In a sort of breathless voice she described him (and these were her exact words) as the greatest athlete she'd ever seen, living or dead, and asked if I'd be willing to do a story on him.

Well, I didn't know how many dead athletes she'd seen performing, but I said I might be willing to take on this hazardous assignment if the pay was right. I said that covering a rodeo was dangerous, especially for the writer.

She never paused. She just bit off that piece of fiction and knocked my price up $750. I mean, this girl was carried away.

But there was another girl who almost got carried away. Linda said they wanted to use illustrations for the article and could I take a few pictures to guide the artist. Since I'd just as soon touch a live snake as a camera I said, no, I couldn't, but that my wife fancied herself a photographer. I said she could handle it.

This is my third, last, and present wife. She is also a Connecticut Yankee who'd never been to a rodeo. When the bull riding started I stuck her out in the middle of the arena with her camera. I had already taken her behind the chutes and given her a close-up look at the bulls. She'd looked at the animals and then she'd looked at me. I could see the calculation in her eyes. She'd been saying, to herself, "I have married a man who used to ride these beasts. Or try to. I have married a crazy person."

It went all right for her out in the arena. The closest she came to getting horned by a bull that was trying to kill her was at least a foot.

Later she confessed her feelings toward me after she'd first seen the bulls. I'd said, "Oh, I'm the crazy one, right? Because I used to be a bull rider. But I guess I'm not the one who, armed only with a camera, and never having been to a rodeo before, or seen a rodeo bull, went out in the middle of that arena."

We'd been married less than a year at that time and I thought it important to shut her up good. Worked, too. I know because she didn't speak to me again for a week.

On the platform above the bucking chutes, the rodeo announcer, Don Endsley, is saying: "And now, ladies and gentlemen, we come to that premier event in rodeo, the one you've all been waiting for—cowboy bull riding."

In the outdoor arena in Weatherford, Texas, the crowd of some 8,000 stirs expectantly, because this *is* mainly what they've come for. They want to see a 150-pound cowboy set himself down on a one-ton beast made out of muscle and gristle and bone and horns. And win.

Endsley says, "But now let me direct your attention to a very important gentleman who is stepping into the arena, Leon Coffee. Through the evening you've heard Leon and me joshing with one another. Now is the time when he's fixing to earn his paycheck. We've kidded around earlier, but now they've run the bulls into the chutes. And this is the most important part of this intrepid gentleman's job, protecting the cowboys who will be attempting to ride these bulls, and, in some cases, saving their lives.

"Leon, take a bow.

"I didn't mean that low a bow. Leon, get up out of the dirt. The bulls will have you there soon enough, and get up here by the chutes and watch over these cowboy bull riders.

"You said what?"

In rodeo, during the repartee between the announcer and the clown, the clown cannot be heard by the crowd, so the rodeo announcer speaks for him.

Endsley recaps: "You say you're going to quit? That you're leaving town? Why, Leon?

"Because of your mother? Oh, you want to save her a trip to the hospital. Is she sick?

"She's not sick? But if you fight these bulls she'll have to go to the hospital. Why?

"To see you."

The crowd laughs politely.

There are two kinds of rodeo clowns: One performs a routine, often with animals; the other makes sure that the bull riders don't get themselves killed. He is called a bullfighter, and rodeo cowboys believe these superbly conditioned athletes are the greatest bull-fighters in the world. But the public and the media continue to refer to them as rodeo clowns.

Leon Coffee is of the second category. He's 6 feet even and weighs 170 pounds, and in 1983, *American Cowboy* magazine named him Pro Rodeo Clown of the Year. Coffee is the only black rodeo clown on the circuit. He's already 29, and in this demanding profession, he's got only six or seven years left at most.

I know, because I used to be a bull rider myself for more years than I care to remember. Earlier, I'd been with Coffee in his motel room when he was putting on his work clothes. Surrounding him, even at that late moment, were bull riders who were still seeking his advice about the bulls they'd drawn that night.

The best experts in the game have said that Coffee has a "headful of bull sense." In other words, he knows what that bull is going to do before the bull knows. And that's why he's alive today.

"Leon, I've drawn 747 tonight. Brindle bull. What do you think?"

Coffee is sitting in front of a mirror putting on his greasepaint. He says: "Bull is going to come out, make one jump to the right, then cut back to the left and begin to spin. Depends on what chute they run him into. I'll speak to the arena manager and try to get him into a middle chute."

"Leon, I got old 44 tonight."

This is from Bobby Del Vecchio, a cowboy from Bronx, New York.

Coffee turns around to him and laughs and says, "Man, you in a lot of trouble."

"C'mon, c'mon."

"First place, bull ain't going to give you no show for the money. Second, he going to try and kill you when you come off him."

What Coffee is talking about is the paradox of the bucking events in rodeo. In those three events—saddle bronc riding, bareback riding and bull riding—you are judged 50 percent on how well you ride the animal, but also 50 percent on how well the animal bucks. It's a factor you have no control over. You can put the best ride in the world on a bull, but if he doesn't buck you are not going to the pay window.

We arrive at the arena where, just like a matador getting out of his car at the *corrida de toros,* Coffee is immediately surrounded by children and fans who want his autograph. Even though we are running late, he patiently signs for everybody, including a rodeo groupie (in my day called a Shiny Bright, but now known as a Buckle Bunny) who opens her shirt and asks him to sign on her bra.

All Coffee says, as we walk toward the chutes is, "Man, I'm glad she had something on underneath her blouse."

Coffee came to rodeo the way most cowboys do: He was born into it. His grandfather owned a 1,500-acre ranch, and his father broke and shod horses in Blanco, Texas, about fifty miles west of Austin. As a kid, Coffee liked to ride bareback, the wilder the horse the better. At age nine he began competing in rodeos. But after fourteen years, he says, "It wasn't a challenge to me anymore." So instead of dancing on a bull's back for a living, this cowboy started disco dancing in front of the bull's face—to the tune of *I'm Your Boogie Man* by KC and the Sunshine Band. "That's my trademark," he says.

But the job isn't all Saturday-night fever. He goes to the stock manager and questions him about the bulls. He already knows the stock, but he leaves as little as possible to chance. That's one reason he's among the best.

The program begins with either bareback riding, steer wrestling, calf roping or one of the other events that keep a crowd in the stands while they wait for the bull riding.

During that time Coffee is out in the arena clowning around with a calf rope. He's lassoing women barrel racers after they've finished their ride, bucking-event cowboys who lean up against the chutes and J. G. Crouch, his partner at this rodeo.

Crouch is not a bullfighter in the sense that Coffee is. He does a dog and donkey act, but he has fought bulls, and tonight he'll use a barrel to distract the bull and to protect Coffee.

Weatherford is an old, classic rodeo, featuring the best cowboys and stock. When it's finally time for the bull riding, Coffee walks up to the chute gate where the first cowboy will be bursting out. Coffee asks him if he knows what the bull is going to do and inquires whether he wants the animal to be taken in a certain direction.

But as Coffee looks over the bull rider, his attention is drawn to the way the cowboy has wrapped the rope over his hands. A bull rope is a flat, braided piece of line that a cowboy runs through a loop and then wraps tightly around his hand. The bull rider, with the help of partners standing on a little platform behind the chutes, tries to pull the bull rope just tight enough for the particular bull he's riding. Put too much of a strain on the wrong bull, and by the swell of his muscles, it'll take that rope out of your hands faster than a heartbeat. If the rope is too loose, you'll be trying to ride off the bull's side one jump out of the chute.

Some cowboys take death grips, trying to glue themselves to the bull by making two wraps around their hand or running the tail of the rope between their ring and little fingers. "And that just naturally scares the daylights out of me," says Coffee.

It should, because if the cowboy bucks off "over his hand," it is going to make Coffee's job of freeing the cowboy that much more dangerous. A rider who gets "over his hand" is thrown forward by the bull in such a manner that his hand twists in the rope and he's hung up beside this giant bucking animal, jerked around like a rag doll and unable to help himself. That's when Coffee has to grab the tail of the bull rope, unwrap the cowboy's hand so that he's freed and then present himself to the bull as a target to distract it from the fallen cowboy. Unfortunately, this most often happens when the rider has gone into "the well," which is what the cowboys call the inside circle of a spinning bull. These days, most professional rodeo bulls are spinning bulls because those are the only ones you can win money on.

Nothing very spectacular happens on the first three bulls out of the chute. Coffee is right in front of them as they explode, slapping them this way and that, controlling them as the riders have requested. But he's worried about the next contestant out, a young rider from Weatherford named Nicky Hite, who hasn't had much experience. Hite has drawn A-16, a bad bull to buck and a bad bull to fight.

This time it goes all right. Nicky is putting a good ride on A-1o until the tie-down on his left spur breaks and he slips off the side, landing on the ground like a heap of laundry. Coffee comes swooping in to take the bull away, and Nicky makes it to the fence.

Now back down in the arena, Coffee and I are talking during a brief break. Sweat is streaking the clown-white makeup on his face. He says, "Man, I don't need any more like that. Maybe the rest of the bulls will be rocking chairs."

But it's not to be. On the sixth bull is Mike Collier, who earlier had asked Coffee about 747. Perhaps because of mixed communications between Coffee and the rodeo stock manager, the bull has been put in the wrong chute.

As Coffee had predicted, it comes exploding out of the gate, makes one jump, then heads for the left-hand corner of the arena and goes into a spin. Coffee tries to slap it back to the right, but the bull has its mind made up and a rodeo bull isn't easy to distract when it's going about its business.

Then, the worst thing that could happen in that tight corner happens. Collier bucks off over his hand and is hung up. Suspended by his hand, he is being jerked up and down with such tremendous force you wonder that his arm doesn't come loose at the shoulder. Somehow Coffee skirts the bull's horns and throws himself across its back. He grabs Collier's wrist with his left hand and, with his other hand, grabs the tail of Collier's bull rope. Somehow, faster than you can see, he unwraps the cowboy's hand. The cowboy falls free. But Coffee, who must now lead the bull away from Collier, falls from its back slightly off balance and the bull, coming around in his spin, gives Coffee a terrific thump in the ribs with the flat of its horn. Coffee keeps his balance and, with the help of J.G., they lure the bull back into the middle of the arena where the pickup men, on horseback, can run it out the gate.

But Coffee is hurt, and he needs a second to collect himself. Endsley sees this and goes into a spiel about what a terrific performance they've just seen by the premier bullfighter in rodeo. He ends by saying: "Leon, take a bow." Coffee is hurting too much to take a bow, though. Instead, he doffs his hat to the applauding crowd and turns a painful grimace into a smile.

For the grand finale, they turn out a riderless bull for Coffee to play with. Coffee cuts a few didos with it, but the bull won't cooperate. It wants out of the arena, and it's staying along the fence. Coffee wants to jump over the bull's horns, but the bull won't be maneuvered into a position that gives him a clear shot.

"What the hell," he says, and signals to Crouch, who nods and leans over slightly, the top of his hat six feet from the ground. Coffee makes a few half circles and then runs at his clown colleague—and jumps straight over him, kicking off J.G.'s derby with his left foot as he flies by. Not bad, considering all that loose dirt and a possible broken rib.

What with the well-wishers and the autograph seekers, it takes us an hour to get out of the arena. Finally we are back in Coffee's motel room, and he sinks down on the side of his bed. He is so weary that it takes him a minute to kick off his baseball spikes and another minute just to remove his socks. When he gets his shirt and jersey off I see the huge welt on his ribs that the bull has given him as a going-away present. But Coffee's felt worse than this. He has broken his neck, his back, both collarbones, both wrists, one leg, one foot, and half of his ribs. He has also suffered several penetrating horn wounds. And then there's his crooked grin, compliments of a bull at the Dallas rodeo that tried to drive his face from the right side to the left side with its horn. As a result, the right side of his face is mostly plastic and wire. They carried Coffee out of the arena unconscious that time, but within minutes he was back on the job.

Taking his makeup off, he says, "Bad bulls tonight. Bad bulls." Then he shows me that lopsided grin and says, "But, hey, man, they all bad."

So I finally have to ask him the question that I already know the answer to, but you don't.

"Why, Leon?"

He laughs slightly. "Because the money's good."

It's a reasonable answer, because Coffee is making about $80,000 a year. But it's not the truth.

So I say, "No."

He looks around at me from the mirror. "Because I like the applause?"

"No."

Then his eyes sort of flash and he says, "Because I like people, and bull riders are damn good people, and I don't want to see them get hurt any more than they have to."

And there you have it.

12

Larry, the White Water, and Me

Larry Peccatiello was down in my city a little while back to speak at a coach's clinic and he read this story. He denied, to my wife, that it happened the way I have described it here. I have run white water all over this country and the only white water Peccatiello had ever seen, prior to our trip, was in a whirlpool bath.

Yet he had the gall to question my veracity in front of my wife. Here and now I call him a liar.

One of the problems with being friends with big-time football coaches is that all they do is talk about football.

And this long after your own pigskin days are over. And you know it and it hurts. But they don't care because they are still close to the game.

Well, maybe I did overemphasize Peccatiello's ineptitude.

But he had it coming.

O n the surface this is going to seem like a story about the friendships that develop between sportswriters and big-name coaches and the problems that can cause. Something like mixing business with pleasure.

Well, that is not what this story is about. This story is about when Larry Peccatiello, now the defensive coordinator of the World Champion Washington Redskins, almost got me killed on a canoeing trip through the white water of the Guadalupe River in Texas.

I may mention something about that friendship business later, but first I'm going to tell you why a man with that many championship rings should not be allowed in the bow of a canoe.

Certainly not in white water.

I'd known Larry since about 1970, when he was with Rice University. On the occasion of this canoe trip he was the linebacker coach of the Houston Oilers.

He wanted to take a canoe trip. Well, that sounded pretty good. Peccatiello had always been good copy for me and I figured I owed him. Besides, he was a big, strong man of good character, reacted positively under adverse conditions, understood the necessity of teamwork, and came highly recommended by himself.

Besides, we weren't going to run that savage a stretch of water. I'd planned a fairly gentle two-day run of about sixty miles, some of it training water and some of it, depending on the season, rapids that can get a little dicey if you're not reacting as fast as you should.

We started off down a nice gentle stretch of training water and I carefully explained to Larry that the stern man commands the canoe, but that the bow man is riding point and must instantly respond to the stern man's commands. I explained really complicated stuff like, "If I yell 'paddle on the left,' that means paddle on the left." And vice versa. Or, "If I yell crossbow right that means you've got to get that paddle sideways in the water and give me some drag on that side."

Stuff they teach at girl's summer camp.

I also very carefully pointed out (it seemed a little unnecessary at the time, although not on reflection) that he had a better view of upcoming water from the bow of the canoe than I did in the stern. A fact I thought self-explanatory.

All this time he's grinning and saying, "Yeah, yeah, coach. Gotcha. Piece of cake. Hey! We'll ace it."

Peccatiello is from New Jersey and he says "Hey!" a lot.

We got started. Went ambling along. Nice day in late May. Came the first stretch of faster water and Larry did pretty well. Responded to commands from the stern, knew his left from his right, even kept his eyes up river. I was beginning to have confidence. I'd taken some novices down some fairly rough stretches of water and none of them were near the physical specimen Larry is nor anywhere near as personable.

Which is the last time I'll ever choose a canoeing partner based on his personality.

It came late afternoon. I could see the river narrowing ahead and I could hear that distant roar that should warn any canoeist. But Larry and I had been talking about the play of an Oiler linebacker and Larry had been mouthing him down. I'd said I'd thought the guy had played pretty well. Larry turned around to me and said, "Hey, coach! We don't pay them to play, we pay them to win."

About that time we swept around a sharp bend in the river and hit the roar that had been magnifying. The roughest stretch of water with stumps and rocks and trees that we had seen yet. Peccatiello was still looking back at me. I yelled, "Hey!"

Meaning for him to pay attention and put his attention forward.

He said, "Hey! Gotcha. I'm telling you the man can't play in the NFL."

At that instant I saw the biggest cypress tree that God ever created right out in the middle of that river. I yelled, "Crossbow right!"

Because I somehow had to find a way through the sweep of water I could see swirling around that tree.

But all Larry heard was me say, "Right!"

So he looks back at me and says, "No point in arguing, right?"

I have run the Rogue River in Oregon. I have run some stretches of the Rio Grande that make strong men quail. I have been bounced around and battered about as bad as you can be in an aluminum canoe in white water.

But I will guarantee you that we hit that tree, dead in the center, as hard as it is possible to hit anything in a canoe short of going over Victoria Falls. Suddenly the canoe was upside down and Larry and I and everything else were in the water. Swift, swift water.

Fortunately, it was only about four feet deep and contained no more rocks than a granite quarry. Peccatiello and I finally struggled over to the bank. For a good while we just sat there and panted. Finally I looked at him and said, "Oh, yeah? Piece of cake, huh?"

He spread his hands in that engaging way people from New Jersey have, and smiled that engaging smile that NFL coaches have, and said, "Hey! What can I hear with all that water making all that noise? I just thought you were saying okay."

With as little homicidal bitterness as I could manage I reminded him that I'd explained that *loud* water is *bad* water and that his job was to keep his eyes ahead and warn me of obstacles.

His answer? "Hey, what does a guy from New Jersey know from trees in the middle of a river?"

The canoe—now with a bent prow—had fortunately beached itself downstream about a hundred yards. We went down to examine the remains. Almost everything was by now about a mile and a half downstream: provisions, matches, ice chest, extra clothing. Stuff that I had lashed down so well I wouldn't have believed it could be dislodged.

But we'd managed it.

What we were left with were two sodden sleeping bags that now weighed approximately three hundred pounds apiece. Fortunately, two of the four paddles I always carry had also washed up on shore and we found them after some searching.

We stood there looking at each other. We were in the big middle of nowhere; wet, out of everything, with nothing but a bent canoe and two paddles. Larry gave me this big, hopeful smile and said, "So . . . . What do we do now, coach?"

He was lucky. If I'd had a gun it would also have washed downstream.

I said, somewhat grimly, "We paddle."

"Hey! What do we eat? How do we build a fire? What about dry clothes?"

I said, "We paddle. And we paddle hard. And you better keep your head up river."

What he didn't know, but I did, was that about ten miles upriver was a boy's camp whose director was an acquaintance.

Well, acquaintance is too kind a word. We had faced each other across a tennis net on several occasions and we each held certain opinions of the other. But even in that season and even in those climes, a night in the woods in wet clothes with no food is rarely preferable to a damaged pride.

So we paddled. We were in a section of the river that was fairly docile, but even so we just barely made the landing at that boy's camp as night came on. Leaving Larry at the canoe, I made my way to the director's office, looking like I'd just been washed down the river, and faced him.

It wasn't too bad. All I asked for was a night's lodging and some food and as little humiliation as possible. When he found out I had a Houston Oiler coach with me, the food and lodging were easy. Larry made a campfire talk to the boys to great acclamation and autograph signing.

Guess what I got from the director.

Several snide looks and, "Thought you were supposed to be such a hotshot in a canoe."

But I took it, I took it. I figured that Larry would straighten him out if the opportunity presented itself.

Must not have.

We made the rest of the trip the next morning in relative calm and I thought that was the last of it.

The man made a mistake, the man knew it, and the man would never say another word on the subject.

Now, about that special relationship that comes from friendships between sportswriters and coaches. The relationship is basically adversarial. You want them to tell you things they don't want to reveal and they want you to print stuff that is of no value to your reader. Ad infinitum.

Then you get a friendship going with one and the whole ballgame changes. He's willing to tell you intimate matters in sport that you'd give your liver to use, but you can't. Because of the friendship. It's not a "this is off the record" situation, it's more like confidences between best friends. They *know* you won't use it because it might hurt them or their team. During Peccatiello's moves from the Oilers to the Seattle Seahawks to the Washington Redskins, he told me some inside information I would have killed to print.

But I didn't. That's the kind of guy I am.

Now having said that, let me tell you just how faithful Peccatiello was to our friendship pact.

I saw him during a recent coach's clinic and he was telling and retelling anyone close enough to listen about that unfortunate canoe trip. In every recounting it was my mistake that caused us to hit that tree and it was only through his heroic and tireless efforts that he was able to drag my near-lifeless body to the bank and then search through the night for aid and sustenance.

So much for the popular misconception that coaches and players are always misquoted by the media. And so much for that pact of silence that sometimes occurs between sportswriters and coaches.

Larry Peccatiello is a hell of a defensive coordinator. Just don't ever get into a canoe with him.

13

The Birds of Death

There is a curious prologue to this story. About three days prior to going down to Mexico for the cockfight, I'd had occasion to punch a gentleman in the face. Unfortunately I caught him with an uppercut, an uppercut that broke off one of his front teeth and caused it to lodge in my knuckle. Now I didn't know I could hit that hard, but, apparently, I'd hit him hard enough to drive that tooth deep enough into my first knuckle that I couldn't see it.

Came the day to go to the cockfight I was running a pretty good fever and my hand was starting to discolor. I didn't think much of it, thought I'd just bruised it and, given time, the problem would go away.

But I was so weak and giddy that I hired a cab driver to take me over to Mexico for the cockfights and to stay with me and then bring me back. It was well that I did because, by the end of the evening, I was so fuzzy I could barely stand up.

Nothing against the hospitals in Laredo, but I knew a good orthopedic surgeon in Kerrville and I somehow made the 180-mile drive to see him. A Dr. Ray. He took x-rays and then told me matter-of-factly that the reason I had such an infection in my hand was that I had a human tooth lodged in my knuckle. He went on to tell me just how infectious the human mouth was.

So much for kissing.

The upshot was that Dr. Ray removed the tooth (an experience I'd liken to having your foot pulled off) and then I spent a week in the hospital while the doctor talked enthusiastically about also removing my hand, which by now had turned black.

I wrote this story with my typewriter propped against my knees, left-

handed, with my right hand suspended above my head and an IV in my arm.

I don't type well left-handed and I have resolved, since that time, that if I ever hit anybody again I'm going to protect my right.

By the way, the only thing that kept me going during that very bad time was remembering the look in that fighting cock's eyes when he wouldn't quit.

Corny but true.

The four matches had been made for 5000 pesos each. They were between Fernando Solís and Antonio Chapa, the two best breeders in Nuevo Laredo. If it had been bullfighting it would have all seemed matter-of-fact. But it was not bullfighting, it was cockfighting and it was illegal.

The last fights of the season had been held in the interior of Texas, and now the only action a cockfighter could hope for until the fall was along the border. Which was not so unlikely: though Texas has perhaps more cockfighters and breeders than any other state, the headquarters is in the border country. It is looked upon there almost as a national sport, and Mexicans and Texans fight their birds freely across the Rio Grande.

But the match had begun badly for "Nano" Solís, a young man of twenty-eight who looks enough like a bullfighter to be one, with his slim size and handsome sculptured dark face, his jet-black hair and flashing white teeth. It had begun badly because he had put his best bird, a purebred Spanish cock named Pepito, in the match in hopes of shaking his opponent's confidence. But Pepito was in trouble. Three times the two cocks had been pitted, faced off across the line drawn in the hard-packed dirt of the little ring, and three times Nano's handler had had to take Pepito up lest the referee call a win for the opposing cock. Now Pepito had a broken left leg and his right eye was swollen almost shut. The handler walked around the ring with him, cradling him in both arms, taking mouthfuls of water and spraying them down Pepito's back, trying to cool him, to give him new life.

Outside the ring Nano looked worried. Even though he was a professional cockfighter, 5000 pesos was a great deal for a man of his poor means to bet on each match, and he had counted on Pepito winning this first one.

And it would be a hard thing indeed to lose Pepito. Pepito's sire was dead, killed in a fight at one of the big *ferias* (fairs), and Pepito was the last of the pure Spanish stock he'd imported from Spain. Watching, he now regretted his decision to fight the little red cock, but there was bad feeling between him and the opposing breeder, Antonio Chapa, and he had wanted to embarrass him quickly.

But Chapa had countered with a pinto cock, a brown-and-white-speckled cock of mixed German and Spanish breeding that was jumping higher than Pepito and spurring him about the head. The pinto was, as some boxers are, a headhunter. He had several times dazed Pepito and had closed one eye. They were not fighting the cocks with the long, deadly steel gaffs that are attached to the natural spurs of the birds, nor with the swordlike inch and a half slashers, but with short, blunted steel spurs. It was late in the season and neither breeder had wanted to risk losing valuable battle stock. Nevertheless, a cock could be beaten to death with the short spurs unless the referee stopped the fight in time.

Now, as his handler still circled the ring with Pepito, Nano was considering whether to concede and save his cock or hope that Pepito would make a comeback. The little cock had fought three times before, but he'd won so easily each time that he'd never been really tested.

The crowd and the referee were beginning to yell for the fight to resume. "*¡Pelea, pelea!*"—"Fight, fight!"—they were shouting. And the referee was motioning to both handlers to bring their cocks forward. Chapa, who was handling his own cock, came forward readily, but Nano's man pretended not to have seen. He glanced over at Nano to see what the owner wanted to do, and Nano stared blankly back, thinking.

The fight was being held in an arena, if it could be called that, about ten miles outside Nuevo Laredo. It was reached from the highway over a dirt obstacle course that should have ruined every car that came there. The arena itself was nothing but a tin-roofed shack, open on all four sides. The ring was an enclosure twenty feet in diameter formed by a three-foot-high wall of canvas. Forty or fifty spectators sat just behind the canvas wall in old and rusted metal folding chairs, most of which were imprinted, from some long past time, with ads for Coca-Cola or Carta Blanca or Corona. Nearby, in a booth, a woman cooked *carne asada* and *fajitas* over an open fire, and those at the ring could smell the mesquite smoke and aroma of the meat. The impresario of the establishment, Miguel Martinez, sold soda pop and beer and Scotch whisky from his own booth. He was doing a lively business during the delay, though not so much on the Scotch because it cost 30 pesos (about $1.50 American) and besides, as one spectator told his friend, it was too hot to drink whisky anyway. In the vicinity of the pit there stood a whitewashed ramshackle building that was referred to as the "rancho", and a couple of stripped, rusting trucks sat in the yard, looking as if they'd be there forever. Beyond that there was nothing but baked soil, dry mesquite trees, and chaparral.

Contrary to what most people think, cockfighting is not illegal in all of the United States. It *is* illegal in Mexico, except at the big fairs that are held on certain holidays. It is permitted at the fairs because there the government can collect a tax, or *impuesto*. Miguel Martinez, like all of the operators of the "brush pits," is in a difficult position. Since his business is illegal, he cannot pay the tax, but to exist he must pay the tax. So, instead, he pays a *mordida*, a bribe, in order to be able to pay his tax. He doesn't find it ironic or even unusual. Asked about it, he just shrugged, "Well, that is the way of the thing, so what can one do?"

Miguel had promoted this fight. It had taken some doing because it was so late in the season, but he knew that if he could arrange it, it would draw a good crowd and he'd make money. To attend the fight cost 50 pesos, quite a sum for an afternoon of entertainment in Mexico. And then there was the food and the drinks. Miguel had already made his money and he didn't much care how the matches turned out. As is the custom in Mexico, he put up no prize money. The winnings consisted of bets made by the owners of the cocks. And then there was the betting among the spectators, which was also a private affair. The betting on the match had generally been 100 pesos to 70 in favor of Pepito, and the customers who had bet on him were incensed at the showing he had made. They were beginning to shout curses and insults at the handlers, which was why Nano never handled his own *gallos* (cocks).

"They yell bad things," he said, "especially if they are losing. Certain insults and curses that a man cannot well stand. Sometimes they get drunk and lose their heads and say too much. So I stay out of the ring because"—here he smiled slightly—"I have a little bit of a temper, and if the wrong thing is yelled at me it could be there would be more fights than just the one between the *gallos.*"

Nano has been raising and breeding fighting cocks for about ten years, but fighting them himself for only four. He says he began fighting them to better establish his reputation as a breeder. He presently has about two hundred battle cocks and battle stags (a cock under eighteen months), and he and his wife breed, train, and care for them. Of course not all two hundred of them are in fighting trim. During the regular season he will keep only about twenty *gallos* in training. But now he had to make a decision, because the referee was growing angry, and that would not do. Also Chapa yelled across at him, with an insolent, triumphant look, "*¡Pelea o pagar!*"—"Fight or pay!"

Chapa is ten years older that Nano. He is a fair-complexioned man with reddish hair. He has big shoulders and a bit of a potbelly. He handles his own cocks in the ring because he doesn't care what the spectators shout. Sometimes he shouts insults back at them. He resents Nano because Nano has consistently beaten him.

He shouted at Nano again, and Pepito's handler, still cradling the cock in his arms, looked over at the breeder.

Fernando stared back for a long moment, then slowly nodded.

"*¡Arriba!*" the referee yelled, motioning both handlers forward. The small crowd yelled as the cocks were faced across the line. The big pinto, held by Chapa, strained forward, bristling his hackles. But Pepito barely had to be held. He sagged sideways toward his broken leg. It was not broken at the thigh, but lower, so that the leg was more or less held together by the tough sinew and skin. His eye was still closed, but his head was raised and his good eye gleamed maliciously at the other cock. The referee dropped his arms and the two handlers stepped back. The two cocks leaped at each other. The pinto went higher, vaulting with his back almost parallel to the ground, hitting Pepito with quick one, two, threes, each time they went up. But Pepito was slugging back, going to the body just below the wing, hitting hard with his good right leg and using his broken left more for a guide and a hold. They went up and up and up. Five, ten times. At first the pinto, looking bigger but not heavier, was forcing Pepito back. But the little rooster hung on, socking away with that right leg. Gradually the pinto dropped back until they were even across the line again. Finally they both stopped, squatting on the ground, pecking futilely at each other. The referee made a sign to the handlers to take up their cocks, and Nano's man rushed forward to pick up Pepito and do what he could to revive him. Outside the ring Fernando raised his eyes to the sky as if in prayerful thanks.

In cockfighting, on both sides of the border, the referee is an integral part of the fight. He is responsible for enforcing what few rules there are to the sport (primarily the weight matching), and his word is absolute law. He can, whenever he wishes, disqualify a cock, and bets are paid off on his decisions. He is especially important in fights that are not fought to the death, but to a decision, for the decision is his and his alone. Normally the handlers must instantly bring their birds to the line when he calls for them, but this referee, moving unobtrusively around the ring, was being especially lenient, for he knew that the two cocks had not had a sufficient training period and were tired and in poor condition.

Nano would, however, have to make another decision, though it seemed to him that Pepito had rallied somewhat and he was beginning to wonder if Chapa's cock had as much heart as he might need. But the bettors did not seem worried. Those who had bet on the pinto were now seeking to press their bets with Pepito's backers. There were few takers. In the break there was much laughing and going back and forth to the refreshment stands. Miguel Martínez seemed the most contented man there.

The Mexicans say that their cocks are far superior to those in the United States. American breeders clearly do not agree. A man we will call Morris, from a small Central Texas town, who, like his father before him, has been breeding and fighting cocks all his life, said: "Yeah, I've heard that old story and it makes me laugh. Tell you what, one time I took fifty chickens down to a big fair in Monterrey. Fought forty-seven times and won forty and that was against about as good as they got in Mexico. They say that because they got more foreign bloodlines than most of our cocks do, German and Spanish and Belgian. For some reason they think that makes them better."

Morris is a big, ambling, slow-talking man of some forty-odd years who wrinkles his brow in concentration as he tries to explain about cockfighting. He looks more like a farmer than a cock-fighter.

"There are some other differences, too," he said. "We'll fight cocks within a three-ounce limit of each other, but they'll try to get them right on the nose and even squabble over half an ounce. Hell, I've give away as much as six ounces when I knew I had the best cock. Won with him, too."

Morris keeps some sixty prime fighting cocks on his place, maintaining careful breeding records on the cocks and the hens and leg-marking them so that his breeding lines are exact. He does not cage his cocks as many breeders do but keeps them staked out in a large field. Each cock is leashed by one leg to a twelve-foot cord on a swivel. "That way," he said, "they've got 450 square feet of movement and they're exercising all the time. It also lets them get grasshoppers and bugs and other natural foods that are good for them." Each cock has a tepeelike house with a high roost inside made of stacked-up rubber tires. To get on and off their roost requires some effort since roosters don't fly too well. Mostly they have to jump, which is good for their leg muscles.

The similarity between fighting cocks and boxers is astounding, both in their training and in the ring. In the ring, the slugging, though with spurs rather than fists, is obvious. So is the repeated pitting, which is similar to the system of rounds and which echoes the old-time style of boxing when a man had to "come to taw" (return to a line at the center of the ring). Also, in the shortspur form of Mexican fighting, there is only occasionally a "knockout," and most fights are ended on a decision by the referee.

But it is in the training that the resemblance is most striking. Cocks do roadwork just like boxers. Depending on what type of card he is preparing for, a six-, eight-, or ten-match fight, Nano will begin training that many cocks plus a few more in order to have the required number ready at the time. Two to three weeks prior to the fight, he starts them with three minutes of roadwork, running them around an improvised ring he has on his property. Each day he increases the roadwork up to a maximum of twenty minutes.

"After that much time," he says, waving a hand, "you do not accomplish what you are after, which is the conditioning of the cock. All you are doing is tiring muscles that are ready to fight."

The cocks' legs are plucked up to their bellies, as are their posteriors. A straight line is also sheared down their backs for ventilation, since cocks get hot easily and lose strength by being overheated. During the training period, Nano rubs down the cocks' thighs with a mixture of glycerine and alcohol. He says it makes the muscles more supple. Morris does this, too, though he uses a diferent mixture, which he says is a secret. But he does not run his cocks. Instead he goes out each evening, when they are on their roosts, and gives their leashes just enough of a tug to make them fight and struggle to stay on their perches.

"See, that develops their legs and wings and wind at the same time. I'll give a half-dozen tugs on one leg then switch over to the other one. The good thing about this method is that it really makes them flap those wings and that develops breast muscle, which is important the way we fight in the U.S. with the gaffs. A cock will get hit in the head, but he'll get hit in the breast a lot more, and you want as much meat between that steel and his vitals as you can get.

"Another thing, you don't want any fat in the rear end. I'll take a cock up and feel his behind and if I can feel his gizzard I know he's in shape."

To hold a fighting cock is a surprise. They are hard—hard like well-conditioned muscle—much harder than you'd ever expect a bird to feel.

"Oh, it's muscle all right," Morris said. "You can maybe fry a stag if he's a young stag, but you get one of those three-or four-year-olds killed, all you can do with him is make chicken and dumplings. Always somebody around the pit ready to buy your dead birds for meat. They don't go to waste."

All breeders spar their cocks. They strap on the steel gaffs and on the end of each they stick a small cork ball, much as you would with a foil or an epee. They are sparred to test them for gameness, endurance, and general quickness.

"Sparring," Nano said, "is also very good for the conditioning. After all, the hardest work the *gallo* will do is in the ring, so the more fighting you can give him the better will be his condition. It is the same with boxers, is it not?"

Nano has cocks in a wide range of prices. They are somewhat cheaper in Mexico than in the United States, but they are still expensive as chickens go. His lowest-priced stags will cost a buyer at least $20, and those out of proven fighters will go up to $50 and even $100. He has a few cocks like Pepito that would cost $200 or more—if he were willing to sell them.

"You must not," he said, "sell too much of your best breeding stock or else you are out of the breeding business."

Of course the hens are sold, too. And some of these bring as large a price as the cocks.

"Most people do not understand," Nano said, "that the *gallina* is more important to the breeding than the cock. I test my hens, sparring them against each other just as I do the *gallos*. But the true test of a hen is in the performance of the *gallos* she brings. That is always the test, in the ring."

Morris's run-of-the-mill cocks bring about $50. After that the prices start upward rather sharply, going to $150, $200, and $250. Not all his cocks are kept in the field. Eight or ten are housed in a special shed. These are the expensive cocks, the ones that have won time and time again and have been or are about to be retired to stud.

But in one special run is the true cock of the walk on Morris's place. This is his cock that has fought eleven times and won every match. He is in a large, cool enclosure, surrounded by a little harem of hens. His fighting days are over.

"That cock," Morris said firmly, "is not for sale at any price. I wouldn't take two thousand dollars for that bird. Why should I? He's only four years old and God knows how many chickens I'll get out of him, the least of which will be worth a hundred dollars as stags. That cock is famous. Even if I wanted to fight him again I probably couldn't make a match. No cockfighter is going to put his bird in against that one."

The eleven-game winner does not have a name, nor do Morris's other cocks.

"No use naming them. I just go by their color and their leg markings. Tell you a story about that eleven-game winner. My boy who lives up in East Texas come down to get him, said he had a match for him. Well, at that time he'd won ten fights, and I had firmly decided to retire him to stud. I said, 'Oh, son, don't fight that cock. Please don't fight that cock.' But he said, 'Dad, I've got a match made with this old boy who's got more money than he has sense and it's just too good a chance to pass up. There's not a cock in this part of the country can beat that bird. I've got to take him.'

"Well, of course I let him because I do with my boy just like my daddy done with me, let him use his own judgment. But, I tell you, I stood out in the front yard damn near with tears in my eyes watching that truck drive off.

"But he come back next day with the cock absolutely unmarked.

Had a nice little chunk of money, too. But, I tell you, I took that cock out of the truck and said, 'Buddy, you are now retired!' Said it loud, too, so everybody could hear me."

Most matches are individually made. A handler takes as many cocks to a fight as he thinks he can match and then goes from breeder to breeder looking for a fight and a bet for his birds. Such matches are called "brush fights" because they usually take place out in the country on someone's private property. The other type of fight is the derby, where a promoter makes the match-ups and there are entry fees and prize money. There may be as many as two or three hundred spectators at a derby, and the betting is fast and heavy with wagers in the thousands.

Morris pointed out a white cock with a few brown markings. "Now this cock fought the longest fight I've ever been involved in or ever seen. I don't know exactly how long it took, but we started in the afternoon and was fighting in this little brush pit that didn't have no lights. Well, it come on and got dark and those birds were still going after it. Now my cock is white and the other bird can see him, but mine can't because the other bird is a dark brown. So all my rooster could do was counterpunch. Every time that other cock would hit mine, this little white cock would hit back. Pretty soon my cock got in a good lick and this other bird let out a squawk. Well, that done it. That other bird went to squawking and my bird was finding him by sound. Chased him over in the corner and killed him."

Morris, like most breeders, gives his cocks a shot of the male hormone testosterone seventy-two hours before a fight. He says it increases their gameness. He also gives them a shot of some secret preparation fifteen minutes before they go in the ring. He says it stimulates their hearts.

"I've been offered a hundred dollars for that formula, but I'm not about to tell anyone. It's not anything so really special. You can buy most of the ingredients from the drugstore. Course it helps if you know a friendly vet."

There is probably little mystery to the shot that Morris gives his cocks. It is common practice to give the birds a shot of digitalis to stimulate the heart just before they fight. Many of the more sophisticated breeders give their birds shots of vitamin K to make their blood clot faster, so that when they are wounded by the gaffs they will not bleed to death. And, of course, all breeders feed their cocks a high-protein diet. Their diet is quite different from that of ordinary chickens, even to the addition of vitamin supplements to their water.

Cocks fight their best during the breeding season, and most cockfighters capitalize on this by depriving the cocks access to the hens while they are in training.

"They get very fierce then," Nano said seriously. "Sometimes they get so tensed up they will try to peck me, which is almost unheard of. And there are some, who know about such things, who give their *gallos* some medicine that makes them desire the hens even more. But I don't do that. I do not have to."

It is not considered unethical to dope a bird. Even though there is an official cockfighting association, there is not a great deal of control. Anything goes that you can get away with. For instance, since the cocks peck each other about the head, some handlers will put poison on their cock's hackle feathers so that the other cock, pecking there, will become ill.

The gaffs are slightly curved surgical steel weapons that look like large needles. They are supposed to be perfectly round. "But some old boys," Morris said, "will file an edge on the bottom side. If that diamond-shaped gaff hits bone it will penetrate and likely break the bone, whereas if it's round it will just generally slide on off. You've got to watch for everything in this game."

The cockfighting season begins, depending on the climate of the locale, in late fall and usually ends in midsummer. This is because the cocks molt during the hot months, and the molting makes them feverish and weak and therefore unable to fight. Of course, some cocks do not shed as much and do not get as sick, and some breeders have a few cocks on hand that are available for hack matches, which are impromptu fights between two breeders.

Even though it exists freely in Texas, cockfighting is illegal here. Laughing, Morris explained how it works: "Well, we don't exactly rent the auditorium downtown to hold these things, you know. Mostly some old boy will have a pit out on his place in a barn or some such—a place that will maybe hold fifty or seventy-five spectators. Word gets around through our associations and we have a fight. Then a lot of our fights are scheduled ahead of time in our monthly newsletter.

"Course you've got to remember that the local law has more important things to do than run around chasing a bunch of old boys fighting chickens. Occasionally, though, some bunch will get all lathered up, and the sheriff will have to make a raid." He shrugged his shoulders. "When that happens you just pay your fine and charge it up to the price of doing business. No big deal."

Cockfighting is, however, legal in Louisiana. This is because there doesn't happen to be a law against it, a fact which was discovered when a sheriff once raided a pit and brought in fifty or sixty defendants and the judge couldn't find a statute against it. Louisiana is also where the "world championship" of cockfighting is held, in the little town of Sunset. It is a derby. In it a man will fight eight matches with eight different cocks. The entry fee is usually $150 per man, there are about thirty breeders who enter, and it is generally winner take all. The winner is the breeder who wins the most fights, which usually means winning all eight, a difficult thing indeed.

Morris said: "Best breeders and the best cocks in the country. A man has got to have an awful lot of birds to come up with eight of the best because all some hotshot has to have to knock you off is one topflight cock and you're a blowed-up sucker." He looked thoughtful for a moment. "I come close one time. Won seven out of eight. Of late they've started paying more than one person the money, but I'd rather just see the winner get it all."

Morris, like all breeders, has no feelings about whether cock-fighting is cruel or not. He said: "I don't think about it one way or the other any more than that guy who raises meat chickens wonders if it's cruel when he goes to slaughter and process them. I won't deny I love it, and I won't deny I get a thrill out of seeing a game bird fight, but I'll leave the question of cruelty to others."

It is difficult to say if it is a cruel sport or not. On the one hand, a meat chicken, a capon, is slaughtered at anywhere from eight to ten weeks. On the other, a gamecock will not even be fought before he's one year old and, during that one year, he will receive excellent care. And then some cocks, like the eleven-game winner, are never killed, but die a natural death. Many are retired to stud after only three or four wins. The question seems to be whether it is less cruel for the cock to be killed by a man rather than by another cock.

Cockfighters say that the humane societies would like to see the breed outlawed so that it would vanish. To some this makes about as much sense as extinguishing that breed of men who have a penchant for dangerous sports. "The *gallos*," said Nano,"were fighting long before man took an interest in sparring them. It is their nature just as there are various natures of men."

A gamecock's aggression is directed only at another gamecock. A man can hold him, touch him, handle him, and he won't make the slightest attempt to peck. A dog or cat can play around him and the cock will ignore it. Several breeders said that a fighting cock will not even bother a barnyard rooster.

"Beneath his dignity," one said. "He'll just ignore him. Course, it damn near will scare the feathers off that barnyard rooster and he'll find business elsewhere in a hell of a big hurry."

Nano says that he does not feel anything personal for his cocks, that it is a business, the way he makes his living. Yet he does something few other breeders do—he names some of his birds. He named Pepito long before he had his first fight, naming him after his sire, Pepe. He said, "Even when he was young there was something special about him, something rare, and I knew he was going to be very good in the ring. Is it correct to say he had a look?"

But now Pepito did not look well. His right eye was swollen completely shut, and he seemed to almost sag down in the handler's arms. He would react a little when the handler sprayed him with water, but you could almost feel his fatigue. It was as before, the crowd yelling for the fight to go on, the referee motioning the two handlers forward, and Antonio Chapa glaring triumphantly at Nano.

Finally Fernando motioned his handler to bring the cock over. Nano stroked Pepito's head and looked at his good eye. It gleamed back. He studied him, then sighed. "I think he still wants to make a fight. Pit him."

They were at the line again, and this time even the pinto was too tired to strain forward. Yet, when the handlers released them, the pinto still jumped higher and spurred more viciously. But Pepito continued to fight back, slugging the pinto with his good right leg just under the wing, getting in sometimes as many as two or three hits as they went up in the air.

The momentum was slowing, and neither cock seemed able to gain an advantage. It even seemed that the head blows the pinto cock was inflicting were less severe. The two handlers hovered just in the background, ready to take up their cocks at the slightest signal from the referee. Outside the ring Nano looked on, his face impassive. But in the ring Chapa exhorted his cock urgently in Spanish.

They went up again and then again and then a third time. Finally, as if by agreement, they both settled to the ground in almost exactly the place they had been pitted. Pepito was listing slightly toward his damaged leg. But there somehow seemed something different about him. He did not seem so tired. His good eye gleamed and glinted as he glared across at the other cock. The referee motioned the handlers to take up their birds, and they had just started across the ring when Pepito suddenly darted forward and pecked the pinto on the head. Instantly they sprang into the air. But this time it was Pepito that hit first and hit the hardest. A few feathers came floating out from beneath the pinto's wing. The cocks went up again and the pinto did not rise above Pepito for a head shot and again Pepito hit the other with two hard breast blows. When they went up again it was Pepito who was on top, and he hit the pinto in the side of the head with the short, blunt spur. When they landed, the pinto did not jump and Pepito rose above him, spurring now even with his broken leg. Suddenly the pinto let out a loud squawk and turned and ran for the canvas wall. Pepito limped after him and cornered him against the canvas and leaped up, holding him with that left leg and slugging away with his right, jumping on top of him. Two, three, four, five, six times he hit, almost too fast to follow, holding himself in position with his wings, now on top of the pinto, pecking him on the head and slugging away with his spur. The pinto made no attempt to fight back.

The referee hovered over them. Suddenly he threw out his hands like an umpire calling a runner safe, shouting, "¡*Se terminó*!" He reached down and picked up Pepito and held him aloft triumphantly. Those who had bet on the red cock cheered and yelled. Those who had not looked disgusted and blurted insults at Antonio Chapa. Money began to change hands. The referee circled the ring and handed the cock to Nano. He took him, smiling slightly. The cock's good eye still gleamed.

For a second Fernando stroked Pepito's head. Then he looked over at Antonio Chapa and began to laugh. Chapa glared back. Fernando laughed some more, then smiled and turned to put the cock in his carrying case.

It was anticlimactic after that. Nano won the second fight, lost the third, and won the fourth. Then it was over and the spectators vanished as quickly as they had come, jouncing back to civilization over the nearly impassable dirt road. Miguel Martinez began to put up his stock of Scotch and beer and soda pop. The woman who had cooked put out her fires.

Chapa had paid and left, but Fernando was slow to leave. He got Pepito out of his cage and examined the bird's damaged leg and eye. Someone asked if the injuries were very serious.

"Not so very," Nano said: "The leg will mend itself and the eye is only swollen shut, not harmed."

Someone else asked if Pepito would ever fight again.

Nano's white teeth suddenly flashed a large smile. "Oh, yes," he said, "he will fight again. Only now he will fight the hens only. I think he will like that very much." He laughed, enjoying the thought. "Yes, I think he will like that very much."

14

Termite Watkins and the Fatal Pancakes

Ah, poor Termite. He couldn't have beat Howard Davis unless he'd entered the ring with an AK-47. Knocking him out wouldn't have worked because they'd have probably rung the bell and given Davis enough time to recover.

In case you haven't discovered it by now, professional boxing is about as fixed as professional wrestling. Howard Davis was an Olympic gold medalist and he had a contract with CBS. Termite was a nobody, a set-up, a pigeon on the road to Howard's glory.

To his credit, Termite stalked Davis all that evening, trying to land that punch. But all Davis had to do was stay away from him and he'd win the fight. I counted the punches landed and Termite threw and landed many more than Davis. But that didn't make any difference; the outcome had already been decided, as you'll read, when the referee walked into Termite's dressing room, before the fight.

About a year later I took Termite and his wife to a carnival. Termite's luck hadn't changed a lick. It rained cats and dogs.

Talking to boxer Maurice "Termite" Watkins, seeing him, you almost believe he was invented. He's such a perfect type: the street fighter from the rough side of Houston who became a Christian and found the do-right good life. Termite got his nickname because his father was in the exterminating business. He's twenty-three and blond, with classic, unmarked features that belie his fifty professional fights and 137 amateur bouts. He's got success, a great deal more money than most twenty-three-year-olds, a fine family, a beautiful wife, a host of friends. "But I don't know," he said to me. "Somehow I just don't feel right."

This was not long before the most important fight of his career, a match with Howard Davis, the former Olympic gold medal winner. It was after his workout, and his hair was still wet from the shower. "I'm not loose," he went on. "I feel uncomfortable. I'm not even getting edgy. I can't seem to concentrate. I know I can beat Howard if I'm right. I guess it's just this other stuff that's troubling me."

A lot of "other stuff" was going on, but the particular thing he was referring to had happened some six weeks ago when he'd lost his trainer of ten years, Albert Bolden, known in boxing circles as Tater Pie. The split still had Termite puzzled.

"I don't exactly know what happened," he said. "We had a tune-up fight in Beaumont against Baby Perez about six weeks ago. Until about a week before the fight Tater was doing the good job he'd always done. He was making me work, making me train, getting me really tuned up. And then he just quit doing anything. He'd come to the gym, but he wouldn't have much to say. I finally asked him what was the matter, what he was doing, but he said I was doing just fine, just fine."

Watkins paused and looked off into the distance. "I had heard that the people backing Davis had tried to hire Tater to train Howard, but I never believed he'd take it. He hasn't been training Davis, but all of a sudden he just disappeared. He didn't come to my fight in Beaumont, and I haven't seen him since. A guy who's been training me for ten years just disappears. I can't say that Davis's people bought him off because I don't have any proof, but still, it's a heck of a coincidence that he'd just take off like that."

It was turning out to be a very costly coincidence. In desperation Termite's camp had hired a new trainer, something no one wants to do right before such a big fight. They'd picked former Texas featherweight champion Kenny Weldon, even though he had never trained a world-class fighter. Almost unbelievably, he'd changed Termite's style, a style he'd used for ten years. Watkins had been a classic, profile-style boxer, but Weldon had squared his stance after the fashion of Joe Frazier and Rocky Marciano in an attempt to make Termite into a puncher rather than the stylish boxer he'd always been. Weldon thought it would take a swarming, slugging attack to defeat an exceptional boxer like Davis.

But Termite found the new style awkward and ineffective, even against his sparring partners. "I don't feel on balance," he said. "You know, it's basically a hooking stance, and I can hook with either hand, but it practically takes my left jab away from me, and that's always been one of my most effective punches. And I'm getting hit. Good grief, I've never been hit so much in the gym in my entire career.

"I think I'm a better boxer than Howard. I can box with anyone. But Kenny says that isn't the way to beat Davis. We know Davis can't hit, so we figure that if I wade in, I can knock him out. But I don't know about that." He paused and looked at his knuckles. "Howard isn't all that easy to take out, and I hate to look for a win based only on knocking him out."

Then why were they persisting with the new strategy? Why didn't Termite go back to his old style? He shrugged. "When it first came up, my dad, who is my manager, was out of town. By the time he got back it was too late to change. And I've been taught from the very beginning that you listen to your trainer. We hired Kenny to train me, and as long as he's my trainer I'll listen to him. He could be right about what we're doing. We won't know whether he's wrong until after the fight."

But he still looked unhappy.

In the gym the next day he seemed off balance, even against mediocre sparring partners. Watkin's main complaint was that Kenny wasn't finding him any good boxers to spar with. In the past Tater Pie had always been able to come up with good sparring partners. Now there seemed to be a distinct shortage. The only quality boxer Termite could get any work from was Wilfred Scypion, a 160-pound middleweight, 26 pounds heavier than Termite. In Termite's weight division there was only Ronny Shields, a top-ranked amateur out of Beaumont. But he was, as Termite pointed out, still an amateur. "I don't care how good an amateur he is, he just hasn't got the moves and the knowledge that a pro does."

Watkins was also dissatisfied with his stamina training. Weldon had him running only one or two miles every morning, whereas he was used to at least six. "I understand Kenny's thinking," he said. "I condition really fast. I don't smoke or drink, and I keep good eating and sleeping habits, so I get in shape very fast. Kenny says he doesn't want me to peak too soon. But I don't know. Here I am, training for a ten-round fight, and I'm only getting about three rounds of work in the gym. I hope Kenny knows what he's doing."

Four days before the fight, Termite sustained a slight cut under his left eye as a result of an accidental butt by one of his sparring partners. It wasn't a serious injury, but it directly affected his training program. The fight was too important to be postponed long enough for the cut to heal. There'd already been too much promotion, too much interest. And there was CBS to consider. All of this meant that Termite had to curtail his sparring work for fear the cut would be aggravated by another accidental blow. If that happened, of course, the fight would have to be called off.

But there was too much at stake to do that. Fighting has changed in the last several years. Like so many other sports, it has become a commodity. With Muhammad Ali, the promoters and money men discovered they could turn a single event into a worldwide spectacle worth millions of dollars. By the time Ali retired, the public was interested in only the heavyweight division. No other heavyweight could hype a gate the way Ali could, and so the promoters lost their only big drawing card. To hang on to the bucks, they began looking in the lighter weight divisions for charismatic young fighters who could capture the public's interest. Their biggest find was Sugar Ray Leonard, an Olympic gold medal winner and the kind of young man that the public could take to its collective heart. And it did just that. When has any other up-and-coming young fighter been featured on TV in eight of his first twenty-one professional bouts and entered the ring against his division champion as a three-and-a-half-to-one favorite? Leonard is a good boxer, but he's also a product of the hype, the gimmick, the slick sell.

The fight Termite had lined up against Davis was pervaded by the same hype. It wasn't a championship match, but it was typical of the new boxing scene. Davis had a $1.5 million contract with CBS to televise his fights. He was also to get $225,000 for this one fight. If he beat Termite, he'd be groomed for a bout with the lightweight champion, Miguel Espana, which would make even more money for everyone concerned.

For Termite, this fight would bring the biggest paycheck of his career: $45,000. And if he beat Davis, he'd be in a position to negotiate his own TV contract as well as a match against Espana. In addition, he'd already signed a contract with the Summit to fight there at least six times a year, for a percentage of the gate as well as a monthly salary for representing the arena.

So everything was on the line—which made it just that much worse that things weren't going right around the training camp. With two days to go, Termite was becoming concerned that he wouldn't get the referee he had requested, Chris Jordan. Part of the deal had been that he could name the referee and that the judges would be from either Florida or the West Coast. Kenny Weldon had reassured him that Chris Jordan would be the referee.

"But the day before the fight Chris called me and said that he would not be the referee, that it was going to be someone from New York State," Termite recalled. "Well, I went to Kenny and told him, and he said there must be some mistake, that it was still his understanding that Chris would be the referee.

"There I was, trying to train. I thought I had other people handling these details, but they weren't being handled. It started to work on my head—and that's no way to go into such a fight."

Even his wife was worried about Termite's condition. The night before the fight she asked how he was feeling. "Fine," he replied.

"No, you're not," she said. "I can tell. You're not like you usually are. You're not even grouchy like you're supposed to be."

Her comment made him laugh, but it was really too true to be funny.

At the weigh-in on the day before the fight, Termite found out that one of the two judges was from California and the other was from Las Vegas, as was the referee, Carlos Padilla. He tried to protest, but it was too late; everything was already arranged. "I'd understood it was all set," Weldon told Termite. "I've got to admit I fouled up somewhere. I should have been more careful to keep up with all this stuff."

That night Termite reflected, "It really gets complicated. The public doesn't know what goes on behind the scenes, all the little ins and outs. Everyone tries for the edge. It's tough enough to beat Davis when we're on an equal footing, but right now I feel like they've put some moves on us."

Termite had staged a move of his own at the weigh-in. As he stepped on the scales, his father tugged slightly on his trunks, making his weight read 139, instead of his true weight of 134. The contract included a proviso that either fighter would be liable for $10,000 per pound for every pound over 135. So the newspapers published a story stating that Termite, in order to make the weight, would probably spend all night in a steam cabinet. And that, of course, would greatly weaken him.

The thought of the ploy brought one of the rare smiles he wore that night before the fight. "I don't know if they bought it or not," he confessed. "Those New York sharpies who handle Howard know every trick in the book, so I doubt that we fooled them very much. But it still makes me feel good, just knowing we're working on them a little, too."

He and his wife had moved into a hotel near the arena several days before the fight. Unlike most fighters, Termite prefers to have his wife with him immediately before a fight. "Linda is almost a perfect fighter's wife," he said. "She's got great faith in me, she's quiet, she doesn't worry. She's a great comfort." But even with people around him, even with his wife there, he still seemed lonely. He was withdrawn and introspective. Only occasionally did he talk about the next day's fight. At one point he said, "You know, Howard and I talked not too long ago. We're old friends. We were amateur boxers together before he went for the Olympics and I turned pro. I sometimes think that if I'd gone his route it would have been me that would have won the gold medal and then maybe I'd be the one with that CBS contract and all that power behind me." He stopped and halfway smiled. "Did you see us glaring at each other at the weigh-in? Well, we discussed how we were going to act, us being friends. And we agreed that business was business and we'd be friends after the fight. To tell you the truth, I never thought we'd get Howard into the ring. This fight's been on and off for the last six months. But they knew they were going to have to fight me if they ever expected to get a shot at Espana. I guess only one of us is going to come out of this thing going on up."

The next morning he seemed even more withdrawn. He ate a light breakfast ordered from room service and then went for a walk. In the early afternoon Pete Ashlock, who arranges boxing matches for the Summit, came up to talk about what the fight meant to all of them. It was not the kind of talk Termite wanted to hear. He already *knew* what the fight meant, and he didn't need to be reminded. He was polite but distant. But he perked up when Ashlock talked about what marathoners ate the day of a race. He said they ate a lot of starches, like pancakes and spaghetti.

Anyone with the slightest knowledge of athletics would have

known that fighters and marathoners expend different kinds of energy. But Termite knows very little about training methods. And, like anyone about to be exposed to a grueling experience, who has his mind focused totally on his part of that experience, Termite was highly susceptible to well-meaning but misguided advice. So that afternoon, while he was taking his walk, Termite went to Denny's and ate an order of pancakes with syrup. When he got back, he felt overfull and sort of funny. "My stomach gets very small when I'm in training," he said, "and it doesn't take much to fill me up. I guess maybe I shouldn't have eaten those pancakes. It feels like they're swelling on me."

His trainer should have given him strict instructions about his eating on the day of the big fight and, at the least, should have been with him all day and had the proper food ordered. But it was too late to do anything about it now.

About six in the evening, Termite, his wife, his friends, his mother and father, his trainer, and his several cornermen made the trek to the Summit.

In Termite's corner that night would be his father, who is one of the best cut men in the business; Kenny Weldon, who would be the main ring tactician; Tony Gardner, a very experienced and capable cornerman who'd been hired for the occasion; and Clarence Doran, an elderly black who'd worked off and on for the Watkins family for many years but who really knew nothing about boxing. Doran's role would supposedly be only to hand in the stool and the bucket.

In the dressing room Termite went about the business of putting on his ring trunks and his shoes. Then he sat down at the massage table and attempted to read his Bible. But people were bustling around him, making too much noise, acting self-important, distracting the young fighter. Termite was actually the most composed person in the room. At one point he even looked up from his reading and asked in a quiet voice, "Would y'all please kind of hold it down?"

Another distraction was on the way. In a nearly unprecedented action, Padilla, the referee, came into Termite's dressing room to warn him that points would be taken away from him for butting, rabbit punching, low blows, or hitting on the break. Termite and his handlers were dumbfounded. These are standard instructions, traditionally reserved for the meeting at the center of the ring. For a referee to visit a fighter in his dressing room and warn him in such a fashion almost constituted intimidation.

But there was no chance to ponder the intrusion, for it was time to start taping Termite's hands. One of Davis's handlers came into the dressing room to make sure that no foreign objects were concealed under the gauze and tape. Tony Gardner had gone down to Davis's dressing room to oversee Davis's taping on behalf of Watkins.

When the job was finished, the handler wrote his initials on each of Termite's hands with a fountain pen. Then the head of the Texas Boxing Commission came in and did the same. Termite's father tried to enter a protest about the referee's action, but the commissioner just shrugged. "Mister Watkins, these people are from Las Vegas, and they're not really under our jurisdiction. There's nothing I can do about it."

In most fights the people who put up the money for the fight are the ones who call the shots. In this case those people were CBS, Inc., and World Wide Boxing Promotions, which represented Termite Watkins. Howard Davis was the commodity, and his interests were being protected. Just before the fight Kenny Weldon pointed that out. "See, I think we're going to have to knock him out. They've got the fight loaded against us. That's why I put you in the puncher's style."

It was very close to fight time. Termite was shadowboxing, moving around the small room, flicking out his incredibly fast hands. The temperature in the room had been raised so he'd begin to sweat. He likes to go into the ring hot.

Then came the knock on the door signaling that it was time to move to the ring. Termite's entourage, with him in the lead, started down a hallway lined by so many supporters and friends that it took several policemen to escort Termite down the hall, down the ramp, to the arena, and to the ring. He climbed through the ropes and started shadowboxing again. Across the ring, Howard Davis was shadowboxing too. The arena lights were on, and Termite could see the small crowd of 3500, most of them shouting encouragement to him. Ticket prices had ranged from $15 to $100, twice as high as Termite would have liked, since he wanted to fill the place. But Davis's people had insisted on the higher price, thereby effectively limiting the gate and barring many of

Watkins's supporters, who were mostly from the poorer north side of town.

The Davis people had one last ploy on their agenda: Davis's handler had broken one of the laces in Davis's left glove and tied a knot in it. If he had gotten by with it, the knot could have produced some very bad cuts. Instead, it caused a thirty-minute delay while another string was found.

Of all the tricks, Termite was most bitter about the broken lace. "They knew how I warm up. And they knew that the delay would hurt me more than it would Howard, because he starts slowly. So while they were taking that half hour to find another lace, I was getting colder and colder, sitting there with the sweat drying on me."

Once Davis got a new lace, the fighters were brought to the center of the ring and given their instructions. They returned to their corners, Termite scuffling his feet in the resin. The stool was brought out, and the handlers climbed out of the ring. Then the bell rang and it was time to fight.

Termite, in his squared-off stance, looked awkward against the stylish Davis, who was keeping a flurry of light punches going. But Termite, with the faster hands, was also landing punches, and landing them with authority. He won the first round, but he lost the second. Davis, obviously beginning to warm up, scored repeatedly in the third with his rapid jab, and that round looked like a draw.

At the end of round three Termite came back to his corner and told his father and Weldon, "I feel nauseated. I'm tasting those pancakes I ate. I feel like I've got a lump of lead in my belly."

But there was no time to worry about it. The bell rang. The fourth round might have been called a draw, although it looked as if Termite landed the more effective punches. Back in his corner, Termite looked sicker than ever. He told his father, "Daddy, I'm about to throw up."

His father answered, "Son, you can't do that!" even as he held the bucket under Termite's mouth.

He didn't throw up, but Davis's style began to take its toll on the usually tireless Termite, who was obviously feeling the results of his lighter-than-usual training schedule. But he was still punching effectively, even though the squared-away stance kept him off balance. Although Davis was outboxing him, when Termite did land his punches, the other boxer was giving ground.

Then came the decisive sixth round. They were in a neutral corner, Termite desperately trying to trap Davis and punch him out. After a flurry of blows, they clinched. The referee ran in to break them up, and as they broke, both ducked their heads. The top of Davis's head came up and accidentally caught Termite right on the cut he'd gotten in training. Blood began to flow. Every time Davis landed a left jab on the spot, the blood would spatter into Termite's eye.

The situation in his corner was turning out to be an even greater problem, too. Too many people had gathered there and around the apron outside the ring. Clarence Doran, instead of simply handing in the bucket, was now up in the ring, actively telling Termite how he ought to fight. Kenny Weldon was frantically trying to come up with alternatives to a strategy that was clearly not working. Even people outside the ring, who'd jammed their way up close to the corner, were tugging at Termite's leg, yelling at him, giving him instructions. The activity in the corner got so hectic that in the seventh round Tony Gardner, Termite's only professional cornerman, simply retired to ringside and lit a cigarette. "The hell with it," he said. "They don't need me in there. That's not a professional fighter's corner, that's a damn three-ring circus."

By that time it didn't matter, because Termite was not on his game, not able to fight with the straight-ahead stance, the hooking, lunging, punching stance that had been devised for him. His ribs on both sides were pink from Davis's body digs. His face was splotched and red from the jabs and sharp punches. The cut under his eye would not stay closed. By the eighth round it was clear he was losing. His corner had become even more chaotic. Kenny Weldon, unbelievably, began to exhort him, "You got to street-fight him, you got to street-fight him!"

Termite just looked up at him, bewildered. "I don't do that anymore."

Meanwhile his father kept saying, "Son, you've got to dig down, you've got to find a way to win!"

Incredibly, although Termite had been catching a lot of punches in the last rounds, he almost took Davis out in the tenth and final round. He caught him with a good left hook and followed that with an overhand right. Davis was hurt, but acting on advice from his corner, he managed to box and glide his way out of trouble until the final bell rang.

The outcome was inevitable. Termite—sick, using the wrong style, outpowered, outmoneyed, and outpoliticked—had lost. But until the announcement of the winner came, he still danced around the ring, as all fighters do, holding his hands in the air, trying to show how fresh he still was, trying to give the impression that he hadn't been through a tough fight. The crowd cheered.

The decision went to Davis. To their credit, the scoring of the North American Boxing Federation judges made the fight seem closer than it really was. But it still amounted to a loss for Termite.

Back in the dressing room, his people immediately laid Termite on the massage table. The room was very quiet. He lay there, his skin pink from the punches he'd taken, a faint trail of blood trickling down from the cut on his cheek. For a long moment no one said a word; then Termite's father started in on Kenny Weldon about the change in style and what it had caused.

"We lost the fight," he said, "because you fooled around with Termite's style. I told you it was wrong. It was wrong, wrong, wrong!"

Weldon answered, "Look, I was doing the job as best I knew how. You hired me to train Termite and that's what I was trying to do."

But the discussion went no further, because Termite swung his legs around and sat up. "Listen," he said in a quiet voice, "let's delay all this for the time being. We lost the fight, but I don't want to hear about it right now."

That shut everybody up. His father examined the cut under his eye. Pulling it apart with his fingers, he said, "Son, I don't think we ought to suture this. Just butterfly it with tape."

"Whatever you think, Dad. But will someone get me something to drink? I feel dehydrated."

Everyone just stood there, staring at Termite. His father snapped, "This young man's been through a tough fight. Can't anyone around here do his job?"

Clarence Doran hustled to bring Termite a glass of ice water. He drank it all down and asked for another. Then he said, "Dad, I feel really weak and dizzy." So they applied ice to all the pressure points—behind his knees, on his wrists, inside his elbows, on the bottoms of his feet. Gradually the color began to come back to his face.

"I ought to go congratulate Howard," he said. But his father just shook his head. "Wait a while. Take it easy."

After a few minutes they let the press in, and Termite dutifully answered questions. Yes, Howard Davis had won the fight. No, Davis had never hurt him. Yes, he felt he'd hurt Howard, especially in the fourth and tenth rounds. No, he didn't feel cheated by the judges and referee. Yes, he'd like to fight Davis again. Yes, he thought he could beat him the next time. No, the cut hadn't bothered him. Yes, of course, he was disappointed that he'd lost.

After that, his father bandaged the cut, and they let in the friends and hangers-on who'd been thronging the hall. They pressed into the small dressing room, a hundred of them. Their presence seemed to make Termite feel better, but he was obviously embarrassed to see them under such circumstances. The people who crowded into the room didn't seem to mind. They seemed mainly just to want to make him feel better, to tell him how much they thought of him, just to touch him, to have him recognize that they were there.

He stood it, stood the well-wishing, stood the handshaking, the backslapping. But after a time it became too much for him, and he looked around for his father. "Dad?" he said.

Instantly his father said, "All right, everyone out. Termite will see you all later."

And they left. Just like that.

Termite showered and dressed. He was still sitting in the dressing room when Howard Davis arrived, followed by his entourage. They embraced and said the usual things. Davis also said, "I had the luck tonight. I'll never fight you again, buddy. Not ever."

Termite sat up talking with friends in his hotel suite until six the next morning. They did not talk about the fight. At one point his wife left the living room. He followed her and found her about to cry. "No," he said. "After a time we'll get off by ourselves and think about it, and maybe we'll cry then. But not tonight. You're not used to seeing me lose. Neither am I. But we'll get by."

Weeks later I asked him again how it felt to lose such a big fight. "Not very good," he said. "I don't like to lose."

But he would not blame the loss on the maneuvering, the tricks, the game playing by Davis's people. "No," he said, shaking his head, "none of that made any difference. I lost the fight because I didn't beat Howard in the ring. That's where prizefights are won, in the ring."

15

The Perils of Honorary Coaching

Jim Hess ran a sandy on me. In talking to him over the phone about another matter, I'd discovered he'd read some of my books and claimed to be a fan. He wanted to know why I couldn't do a story about Stephen F. Austin University and his football program.

Well, hell, that sounded fine to me, so I said I'd do it if he'd allow me to call a play or two.

As you'll read, three plays got settled on.

I got down to Nacogdoches a week in advance and settled into the coaching routine for the upcoming game. I can now promise you that I would not be a football coach for all the money in the world. I don't mind watching a little film, I don't even mind watching the same play over and over and discussing it to excess.

But I'm not going to do that for nineteen hours a day.

I got my three plays from Bobby Ross, then the head coach at Maryland. Naturally, being a receiver, they were all passes. There was nothing new about them; in fact I don't think there's been a new play invented in football since about 1945. So all three plays matched corresponding ones in the Stephen Austin playbook.

I got to call one of my plays in the third quarter and two of them in the fourth. Funny enough they didn't look a thing like the plays we'd practiced. I don't remember the exact terminology, but I'd tell Jim, "Okay, I want to go with 3-X cross, hound-dog left, rover right."

He'd say, "Fine," and send the play in.

Now 3-X cross, hound-dog left, rover right is a pass play in which the wideouts cross in the middle with the tight end putting a pick play on the right cornerback. If things get a little hot the quarterback has the relief valve of throwing to the fullback on a swing pattern.

But the play I saw was the fullback straight up the middle.

I said to Hess, "Hell, that wasn't the play I called!"

He was down on one knee. Without turning to face me he said, in that mild voice of his, "Quarterback must have checked off at the line."

Same thing happened the next two times. Though in a different way. One time it was an off-tackle play to the halfback and the next it was something equally different from what I'd called.

Hess's answer was always the same. "Quarterback must have checked off at the line."

Well, I took it with good grace until the next day when I was talking to the offensive coordinator, Smitty Hill. Smitty said, "Is that what Hess told you? Hell, he's never allowed a quarterback to option a play since we've been here."

And I hate it because I'm giving Hess this publicity.

---

t was the scarf that did it. The pilot's scarf from the 924th Tactical Fighter Group at Bergstrom (Texas) Air Force Base, of which I'm an honorary member.

But I've gotten ahead of myself. This tale started when I picked up another honorary title, that of honorary coach of the Stephen F. Austin Lumberjacks football team in its 1983 Lone Star Conference football game against the Angelo State Rams. This was a no-joke honor that was bestowed on me because, frankly, I'm a friend of the coach, Jim Hess, as well as a student of the game. I was to be allowed to call three offensive plays. Coach Hess tried to change that to one offensive play and two defensive plays. I carefully explained to him that I knew about as much about calling defensive plays as a pig knows about ice skating. So he'd given in, and I had my three offensive calls.

The Lone Star Conference usually has between thirty-five and forty alumni playing pro football. We're talking Harvey Martin, out of East Texas State, and Wilbert Montgomery of Abilene Christian, who has done a pretty fair job for the Eagles. Then there's Clayton Weishuhn, who used to play at Angelo State and is a very good linebacker with the Patriots. And let's not forget Washington kicker Mark Mosley, who was the MVP of the NFL in

1982. He played at Stephen F. Austin, which is where Bum Phillips, now coach of the Saints, was an all-conference lineman.

Many of the players in the Lone Star Conference were heavily recruited by the major powers, teams such as Texas, Penn State, Oklahoma, and Nebraska. They just chose to stay down home, to play smaller college ball.

Coach Hess called one night in the spring of '83 and asked if I'd like to come down and be the Lumberjacks' honorary coach for the Angelo game. As a player and as a writer I'd seen a lot of honorary coaches. They mostly walked around in three-piece suits and the day before the game were allowed to give a stimulating speech that generally concluded with, "You can do it, men!"

So I declined. "Listen," I said, "I'm forty-six years old, but I still think of myself as a jock. So if I come down there to coach I'm going to *coach.*"

Coach Hess disarmed me by saying, "O.K., we can use the help."

"I'm talking about calling plays," I said.

"How many?"

"Six. Minimum."

That's when we started bargaining, and I ended up with the three offensive plays. I'd have settled for one. But that's life and that's football.

On the Tuesday before the game, Buck, the Stephen F. Austin equipment manager, outfitted me as a coach—I got a pair of shorts, two jockstraps, socks, knit sport shirts, the works— before I took the field and got a look at the players. That's when I decided on the spot to resign. In my own brief and ineffective career as a college football player, I'd never seen such quick and fast and strong young men. Fortunately for me, Coach Hess refused my resignation. He's about as laid back as a pillow, so all he did was laugh and say, "Naw, it'll be all right. We won't get you off in no storm."

He didn't know I already had a history of calling plays. When I was playing at John Tarleton Agricultural College in Stephenville, Texas, Bill Mimms and I were the two left ends who alternated taking in plays. Coaches Sandy Sanford and Joe Abbey were calling the plays. About midseason I noticed that one would call a play and then, just before you ran on the field, the other would grab your arm and change the play.

As I was running onto the field in a game against Schreiner

Institute, I decided that in my considered opinion we didn't pass enough. As a matter of fact, we'd count a forward fumble that we recovered as a completed pass. Well, I felt it was time to change all that. The play I'd been given by Coach Abbey was a 23, the two back up the three hole. When I got in the huddle I told Tommy Hudspeth, our backup quarterback, that the play was 87 Cross. He gave me a kind of blank look for a second and then said, "What the hell is 87 Cross?"

I said, "It's a pass play. That's when me and Puryear cut across the middle about 10, 12 yards deep, and you hit whichever one is open." Bill Puryear was the right end.

Hudspeth said, after a second, "Oh, yeah, I remember that one. On two. Break!"

Well, I caught the ball for about a 14-yard gain and then headed toward the sideline. Coach Abbey and Coach Sanford were standing there with their arms crossed, and just as I got to the sideline, I heard Coach Sanford say to Coach Abbey, "Nice call, coach."

And Coach Abbey, without batting an eye, said, "Yeah, it looked to me like it'd be open over the middle the way their linebackers were dropping off."

This opened up a whole new world for me. I was like an addict after that. We beat Schreiner, primarily on calls I decided on between the huddle and the sideline. Only once did I nearly get caught. Coach Sanford stopped me one time as I was coming back to the bench after we'd just run a sweep and said, "I thought I sent in 34," which was a dive play. I kind of mumbled, "Must have been some confusion in the backfield."

He said, "Yeah, that'll happen. But, doggone, I wish you boys wouldn't forget and get confused. Hell, we practice this stuff all week." Those words about confusion in the backfield were to come back and haunt me thirty-one years later.

Even before I arrived at Stephen F. Austin for my coaching debut, I had my three plays. One I got from my friend, Larry Peccatiello, the defensive coordinator of the Washington Redskins. However, I did check it out with Bobby Ross, the coach at Maryland. It was intended to yield 10 to 12 yards or, if we could hit the flanker, to get us an even bigger gain. The play begins with the setback on the left side going in motion—first heading toward the left sideline and then doubling back to become a lead blocker. Then the quarterback fakes to the fullback up the middle, fakes the pitch to the running back on a right-side sweep and either hits the tight end who's coming across the middle or the flanker going deep, depending on what coverage the defense is in. We called it 124. That was my biggie. But I wanted to set it up with a sweep to the right. For my third play I selected a quick pitch to the tailback, run out of the I formation.

Fine. The Lumberjacks practiced the quick pitch, the sweep, and the 124 all week and they looked good. Only I was getting a little too intense. When the first-string offensive linemen didn't block the way I wanted them to against the scout squad, I'd gotten the bad habit of going over and shaking some of those large people around by their shoulder pads. Coach Hess finally told me, "Why don't you go over there and work with our kicker and punter. Hell, I'm scared you'll hurt some of my little boys."

The man probably saved my life.

Everyone's always talking about how flaky kickers and punters are. Of course they are. Nobody ever pays them the slightest bit of attention. There aren't five coaches in the world who ever kicked or punted a football. Consequently, the kickers and punters are always over there on the sideline by themselves. I know. I was a punter myself.

So I was glad to spend time with the punter, Andy Gamble. We worked a lot on his drop and his coordination and timing, and I told him how Ray Guy used rosin on the right side of his kicking shoe to get more friction on the ball, thereby producing a better spiral. My words would have an effect later.

By the end of the week I felt as if I'd volunteered for a lunatic asylum. The team practiced two and a half hours a day, and the rest of the time the coaches were in meetings, going over the strategy again and again. I didn't get enough sleep that week to add up to a catnap. Some nights we broke up about 2 AM.

Then Saturday finally came. Angelo State came to play. The only things that were keeping us in the game were Gamble's booming punts and some pretty good defense. From our 26-yard line Gamble got off one of 52 yards that, according to my stopwatch, had a hang time of 4.5 seconds. That kind of punting could get you a nice contract in the NFL.

Midway into the second quarter, we finally scraped together some offense and, after a sustained drive, had the ball first-and-goal on their four-yard line. And what does Coach Hess do now? With four downs to make four yards, he calls a pass to split end Floyd Dixon that's overthrown by quarterback Tod Weder. Then he calls a pitch to fullback Michael LeBlanc that results in a fumble. The Rams recover.

It's about 400 yards to the field house at halftime, and I'm right beside Coach Hess and in his ear the whole time. I said, "We're first-and-goal at the four. Four downs! Why didn't you punch it in?"

Coach Hess says, as we're trotting, "I don't know. Give me a break, Coach!"

I said, "To hell with that. We've been running up their middle all night. Why not then?"

He says, "Well, I thought Tod could hit a pass. And we'd get a quick score."

I said, "Oh hell, don't give me that!" At that point Weder—or Weed, as the players called him—was 4 of 12 for 21 yards. He was having a terrible game and couldn't have hit my grandmother on a six-yard down-and-out if she'd been sitting in a rocking chair with no coverage. He'd also lost two fumbles. So I was still in his ear. Finally he said, as we neared the field house, "For God's sake, Coach, give me a break!"

Well, he was lucky. I didn't let up on him because I'd finished saying all I had to say. I was just out of breath.

Coach Hess made a pretty good halftime speech, and Lynn Graves, the defensive coordinator, and then Smitty Hill, the offensive coordinator, both gave their talks. But what I thought was the most effective halftime statement was made by Howard Wells, the offensive line coach. As he was talking to his linemen, he emphasized the point about what a sorry job they were doing by throwing a ten-foot-long Formica-topped table some 12 to 14 feet. Clear across the room. It had to have been a Lone Star Conference record.

That was his second record of the day; about an hour before game time, he'd thrown up three times.

Now it was time for the second half to start, and the handwriting was on the wall. I was standing by the door as the players left the locker room, my fighter pilot's scarf hanging around my neck. The scarf is silk, with small, swept-wing F-4s on a royal blue field.

As the players passed through the door, a few reached out and tentatively touched it. But just a few.

I thought it curious, but I forgot about it because the Rams came right after us. First their freshman quarterback, Ned Cox, wrapped up a 64-yard drive by handing off to running back Eddie O'Brien, who lugged the ball into the end zone. Then they came right back off an interception thrown by Weed. That resulted in a 41-yard field goal by Mike Thomas with 5:07 left in the third quarter.

Angelo State 10, SFA 0.

At that point, I gave up and went and sat down on the bench, hanging my head. But the players didn't give up. Defensive back Kary Cooper, who's about twenty-seven years younger than I am, came and sat by me, patted me on the back and said, "Coach, it'll be all right. Don't worry." And LeBlanc came over, took me by the shoulders, jerked me around and said, "Coach, get your head up! This game ain't over. We're going to beat those suckers."

Then a strange thing began to happen. Almost as if it had been rehearsed, one by one the players began to come by where I was sitting and without saying a word, they reached down and rubbed the end of my fighter pilot's scarf. Early in the fourth quarter, with us still 10 points behind, several players came over, stood me up and pushed me toward Weed, who was standing on the sideline waiting to take the field. I said to him, "I think you're supposed to rub this scarf. I know it sounds silly, but . . ."

He said, "Yeah." And then he rubbed the scarf with both hands.

From then on he was nearly perfect. He took the Lumberjacks on a 69-yard drive, culminating in a 15-yard touchdown run by Ron Jefferson. Rick Wilson kicked the extra point, and it was 10–7.

We held them and got the ball back with 4:30 left, but we were deep in our own territory. That's when I jerked myself together, went to the sideline and knelt by Coach Hess. I said, "Jim, it's time. Run the sweep." He yelled something to Smitty, who was signaling in to Weed the plays that I didn't quite hear. Maybe I had a bad seat, but it looked more like a dive play to LeBlanc than it did a sweep. But it got us a first down.

Then I called 124. I distinctly heard Coach Hess yell that over to Smitty. We got forty-eight yards. Except Weed hit Noble, instead of Dixon, whom I'd designated as the primary receiver. It gave us a first-and-goal at Angelo's nine-yard line.

Two plays and a personal-foul penalty later, we were at their four with another first down. I don't know if this is true or not. I was a little too excited to remember. But Coach Hess swears it happened. He said I was yelling in his ear about us having been on the four once before and having given them a pass look. He said that I told him to give them the pass look again and then run the quarterback draw. Well, somebody called it, because it happened. Weed went straight in for the go-ahead TD.

SFA 14, Angelo State 10.

In the final minute and a half we shut them down completely, sacking Cox three times. And we went into the locker room the winning team, after having been beaten for three-quarters of the game.

Later, at a party at Coach Hess's house, he and I detached ourselves for awhile and went into a bedroom to talk things over. I kind of scratched my ear and said, "Coach, when I called that sweep, to set up 124, it looked like a dive play to me."

"Well, you know," he said, "the sideline is the worst seat in the house."

So I said, "Yeah, but on 124, my primary receiver was Dixon, but Weder hit Noble."

He yawned and said, "Probably a little confusion in the backfield. You know how that goes."

Max Corbet, the sports information director, was in the room with us, and as I walked out, still slightly confused, he said, gently, "Coach Tip, don't you know that Weed has the authority to audible off at the line on every play?"

Coach Hess heard him and hurried over to say, "but don't forget the help you gave us with Andy Gamble." He'd averaged 41 yards a punt.

I was stripped of my moment of glory.

Coach Hess and I had one bad disagreement before I left. He wanted the fighter pilot scarf and I didn't want to give it to him. And didn't. The next week he beat Texas A&I, but then he was to play the Southwest Texas State Bobcats. The Bobcats had what at the time was the longest winning streak for a college football team—twenty-two games—and were also the two-time defending NCAA Division II champions. I sent the scarf in the mail.

At the half we were down 17–zip. Coach Hess later told me he'd hung the scarf on the locker room wall where all the players could see it. During intermission he pointed to the scarf and told them,

"That's a symbol of a fighter pilot. The most dedicated, the most courageous, the most single-minded and goal-directed men in the world. Let every player rub on that scarf, and let every player, in this last half, be a fighter pilot."

With only 4:49 to go, Weder completed a pass to Charlie Smith, who made a one-handed catch, and then ran for a 20-yard TD to tie the game 24-24.

Next defensive tackle Mike Granger intercepted a tipped pass to give the Lumberjacks the ball on the Southwest Texas 36 with 1:47 to play. Five plays later Wilson kicked a 37-yard field goal to make the final score 27-24 in Stephen F. Austin's favor.

Coach Hess called me about an hour after the game, and I asked him what my chances were for getting my scarf back.

He said, "None."

I asked, "What if I offer to buy it back?"

In a firm voice he said, "You don't have enough money and you haven't got any friends that have enough money to buy that scarf back. That scarf is going in the Stephen F. Austin Hall of Fame."

16

X's and O's Revisited

I hate television. In fact I hate the whole electronic media. And to have this happen to me . . . Well, let's just say it was galling.
  Of course Jim Hess played a deleterious role in this debacle.
  I'll get back at him some day.

'm not going to coach football any more. Not that I have coached all that much; in fact, it was just one game. But that was enough for me, and this is my official resignation.

It all began with a phone call from my ex-friend, Jim Hess, the aforementioned coach and athletic director at Stephen F. Austin State in Nacogdoches, Texas. He wanted to know if I cared to be a head coach in what they call the Media Bowl, an intra-squad game played at the end of spring practice for which members of the media take the places of the regular coaches.

Naturally I said yes. There are only two species who take pleasure in second-guessing football coaches: sportswriters and everybody else. Sportswriters are the worst, and I'm no exception. I've never doubted—at least before this—that I could outmaneuver most of those sideline jockeys.

It was an illusion I treasured right up to the moment I took charge of the White team, my half of the Stephen F. Austin Lumberjacks. That's when it dawned on me I didn't know anything about football.

But it was too late for defeatist thoughts. I had to win, and this was more than a matter of honor. My opponent coaching the

Purple team was a member of the detested electronic media, a fellow named Robert Hill. I'm not suggesting that there is the slightest animosity between our two media; maybe I'm just allergic to hair spray.

Of course, before we could play we had to divvy up sides in a draft—the equivalent of recruiting, I guess. The first pick was important because of Todd Whitten, the starting quarterback. The year before, as a junior, he had thrown 27 touchdown passes and was second team all-conference. Winning the coin toss and drafting Whitten was, to me, the key to winning the game.

I tried—I thought with perfect logic—to circumvent the coin toss by pointing out that my opponent had a 2–1 record in the annual game, while I was 0–0. As the coach with the worst record, it stood to reason, I should have first pick.

Hess vetoed that, not surprisingly, but I won the coin toss and took Whitten. Hill got the second- and third-string quarterbacks, and I the fourth. That was the way the draft would go the rest of the way, position by position.

With his first choice, the electronic-media whiz drafted weak safety Darrell Harkless, who was practically All-World and the best athlete on either squad. He was also, I later concluded, very nearly invisible.

As the draft drew to a close and opening practice approached, I grew edgy. These were real live college athletes and I was their coach. I kept thinking nervously, I was supposed to *lead* them. My hands started to shake, and the roster I was holding began to blur before my eyes. My condition was not aided by the genial remarks of Hill, who said, "How can you type with your hands shaking like that?"

I had drafted mainly for the skill positions, while Hill had selected most of the starting offensive line. I managed to get the center and the starting tight end, but I badly needed a starting interior lineman. As I was about to make one of my last picks, a combination of nerves and too much iced tea struck. I assumed the draft would be halted while I excused myself.

I was wrong. When I came back I learned that my assistant, Kevin Gore, a sportswriter for the Nacogdoches paper, had drafted the starting running back, Henry Canady.

A gaffe for sure, I thought, but not desperate. On the whole, the draft seemed to have ended without a conclusive edge to either side. The Purple had the starting offensive line and most of the first-string secondary. The defensive lines were about evenly split, and I had the starting offensive backfield, with an inferior offensive line.

This, unfortunately, was not the way the coaches saw it. They picked my White squad as the probable winner—by 9–1. Talk about pressure. The local TV and radio coverage was unsparing in its admiration for my talent as a picker of football flesh. They hammered away at what a seeming shambles I had made of what otherwise might have been an entertaining contest. Just walking on the field, the White team should light up the scoreboard like a pinball machine.

If I was aware that a certain opposing coach was behind this electronic blitz of encomiums—and I was—I was not tipping my mitt to my players when finally we met for our first practice. Mum was the word about the overwhelming odds. While the regular coaches ran the practices, I stood around nodding my head coolly and looking for that little extra edge I knew I was going to need, no matter what the coaches and those airwave people were saying.

Hess came over to my motel the night before the game, and, looking for a little more power, I said, "How about if I suit up Noble and Dixon?" James Noble and Floyd Dixon were all-conference receivers from the year before who were no longer eligible to play although they were still in school.

Hess gave me a look that scarcely hid his incredulity. "You can't cheat in football," he said. "They got all those guys out there in the striped suits to take care of that." He just shook his head. "You are beginning to sound like one of those coaches you writers are always accusing of evil ways." So I was left to my own humble devices.

In the interim between practice and the game I huddled with my two quarterbacks, Whitten and Todd Hammel, discussing what we wanted to do. Without the good offensive line, I figured, we would have to stick to the short game, dinky passes and dive plays, for lack of blocking time. I would signal either pass or run, and leave it up to the quarterback to select the play.

I planned to leave the defense to my assistant, the aptly named Gore. But I did tell him I wanted to blitz frequently because I felt the Purple team's young quarterbacks would rattle easily.

Sounds like I had a lock on the situation, right? Forget it. First off, I couldn't get my players up for the game. They had begun to believe the hype they were hearing. My defensive tackle, Frank Robinson, said to me, "Hell, Coach, those hamburgers can't score on us. Get down heavy if you can find a line."

What do you say to that? My pregame speech was a failure. I remember mumbling something about "pride" and "executing" and "mistake-free football." I was so bad that safety John Barbe hung back as the team headed for the field. He patted me on the shoulder and said, "It's all right, Coach. We'll get 'em."

Gettin'em at the outset was hardly the problem: survivin'em was more like it. On our first play from scrimmage Canady fumbled. Purple had the ball on our 22-yard line and fumbled it back, but we weren't able to move. Whitten, as expected, wasn't getting time to throw, which meant we weren't getting out of our end of the field. We punted, they punted. They punted, we punted. Purple missed a field goal. We started driving. Canady fumbled—again.

That, for the second time, sent me to the table for water, a trip I would make frequently as the afternoon wore on.

Now, it generally takes a quarterback a little time to catch on to what the defense is doing and how to exploit it. Just as the first quarter ended it appeared that Whitten had glommed on to what was happening, because we were moving.

That's when friend Hess became ex-friend Hess. He came up to me as the teams switched ends and said, "Well, do you want to play Whitten in the third or fourth quarter?"

I said, "Whaaat are you talking about? I want to play him all of the quarters."

He said, "Coach, I can't do that. I told you I was going to have to limit Whitten's play. I can't let him go more than two quarters. Can't take the chance of him getting hurt."

"*Him* getting hurt! You're killing *me*."

I guess I would have been madder, but my freshman quarterback, Hammel, came in and moved the club down the field, and scored on a three-yard keeper. Seven–zip for the good guys.

Well, this was more like it. Coaching, I thought, could be fun.

And it continued to go our way. Tyler Tabor pinned the Purple deep in their territory with a fine punt, and when their quarterback went back to pass, our defensive end, Keith Melcher, got him in the end zone for a safety to make it 9–0.

Then something went haywire. I hate to say where, but I think you're going to figure it out. After the safety, Hammel took us down the field again. With time running out in the first half, we were on the Purple's 10-yard line with second down and goal to go. I took our last time-out, and we had a sideline conference. I wanted a timing pass to the corner of the end zone, with Hammel to throw it away if he couldn't be sure of a completion. That would kill the clock and give us time to get the field goal unit in.

Sidelines are fierce places to try to plot strategy. First of all there is that damn 30-second clock. If you think it's tough on quarterbacks, it's pure hell on the coach who is trying to consider yardage and down and what play to call. And there is always somebody asking you something. Or telling you something. Or just making noise in your ear.

That sounds like just about as good an excuse as any for what happened next. Instead of throwing the timing pass into the end zone, Hammel went to the tight end for a short completion. The end caught the pass but forgot to get out of bounds. Hammel forgot the clock was running and failed to line up the team and throw out of bounds. And I got confused between third and fourth downs and somehow forgot to get the field goal unit on the field in time. It was all one industrial-sized mistake.

The second half was not nearly as confused or as much fun. We had been able to rattle the Purple quarterback in the first half, but midway into the third quarter he started acting like he enjoyed the blitz, because he marched his team down the field and threw an 11-yard touchdown pass to cut our lead to 9–7.

That didn't seem to satisfy him. After Canady fumbled— what else?—this time on our own 20, Kyle Dalton threw for another touchdown.

They missed the PAT, and it was 13–9. I was getting tired of our stagnant nine points. Our punt returner must have sensed that. With a minute to go in the quarter, he took a short, line-drive punt and, behind a good wall of blocking, returned it 73 yards for a touchdown. We missed the PAT, too, but it was still our lead, 15–13.

A field goal, I was uncomfortably aware, could wrest the lead back, but we had Whitten in there. So what was the fear? I shortly found out. We couldn't move the ball. Someone wearing Darrell Harkless's number kept making tackles and either intercepting or knocking away passes. I knew it couldn't be Harkless himself because, when I had protested about pulling Whitten, Hess had vowed he would bench Harkless. And I knew this couldn't be Harkless because I had already seen him for three quarters. No, this had to be some imposter.

But he played an awful lot like Harkless. With time running out the player, whoever he was, intercepted one of Whitten's passes, jumping about eight feet in the air to do so, and the Purple shortly were within field goal range.

I have very little to add except to tell you that they kicked the field goal to go ahead 16–15. We spent most of the final seconds trying to find a place to throw the football where Harkless's double wouldn't suddenly appear. We couldn't find it. The final was 16–15.

I shook hands with the electronic media guy and tried to conceal my disappointment—no, let's admit it, my bitterness—as well as I could.

That night, after the game, Hess and two of his assistant coaches and I ate at an all-night breakfast place. They were in good humor. They had seen positive signs among a lot of their players, which boded well for the next season; they had had a night off; and they hadn't lost a football game. Me, I was experiencing the agony of defeat and doing my snarling best not to let it show.

Clyde Alexander, the coach of the linebackers, said, "Well, Coach, how'd you enjoy the game?"

He did it meanly. I fixed him with a look. "Clyde, there is going to come a game that is lost because one of your linebackers fouled up. Then I'm going to ask you the same question."

Hess said, "Now, gentlemen, don't pick on the man." He giggled. "I don't think he's real happy just now."

"Yeah, Hess," I said, "give them advice. Reduce me to a half a quarterback. Don't even give him time to adjust to the defenses before you pull him on me. And then let Harkless play the whole game."

"He didn't play the whole game. He didn't play any more than Whitten."

Gary DeLoach, the defensive secondary coach, said, "You better look again, Coach Hess. He was in there about every play."

Hess had the good grace to look uncomfortable. He finally said,

"Well, I meant to pull him." And, in the universal language of coaches, added, "I'll have to look at the films."

Hess once told me that after a loss he couldn't stand to read the sports pages or watch a sportscast for several days because he didn't want to read or hear about anybody else winning. I had said I thought that was a pretty juvenile way to act. After all, it was just a game.

When I got home I did not watch TV sports or listen to the radio or read the sports pages for several days. I did not want to read about winning baseball teams, winning volleyball players, winning period. When my wife won $5 in a seed catalog contest, I felt nauseous. I spent most of my time grinding my teeth over the boneheaded way I had botched getting the field goal team onto the field at the end of the first half.

At last, when I thought I could stand the pain no longer, it began to pass. I was becoming civil and even was polite to Hess when he called to say he had seen the film and that, yes, Harkless had been in there most of the game and it was his fault for letting it happen. He said, "Guess he just snuck in there a lot. I should have been watching."

I thought I was over it and went so far as to tell my wife I had been childish. She agreed, I thought, a little too readily. But I let it slide. The game was behind me.

And now I realize I've been using these pages to cry about the sad twists of fortune—something coaches only get to do by talking to sportswriters like me. That's why I quit coaching.

I think I'll stick to having the final word.

17

Of Noble Rites

Every writer has, to some degree, absorbed a great deal of Hemingway. But the problem for a writer who is doing his first bullfight story is to not be over-influenced because Hemingway, by his own admission, was the poet laureate of the corrida.

And it does cause a struggle for the writer to maintain his own style and his own integrity and not fall into the trap of Hemingwayisms. He has a very easy style to copy and the writer doing a piece on bullfighting has to be ever vigilant.

I always thought this was the best short piece of work I've ever done.

In the early afternoon Armillita went to the bullring for the *sorteo*, the drawing and coupling of the bulls. He had to do it himself because he was of the second class of the four classes of bullfighters, and his manager, such as he was, did not accompany him to little bullfights. This one was at Piedras Negras, a Mexican border town across from Eagle Pass, Texas. There was no regular *corrida* season in Piedras Negras. Each fight was a separate entity brought about by the pressure of local aficionados and the courage of some promoter who had been persuaded to take the financial risk. Usually a card featured two matadors of Armillita's class with perhaps a *novillero*. This one, however, was to be an odd contrast since the other fighters were Gaston Santos, a millionaire sportsman who fought from horseback, *rejoneador* style, and Manolo Martinez, one of the four Mexican matadors of the special class, the best. Santos was there because *rejoneadors* are not that important and he would take a *corrida* anywhere purely for the love of fighting bulls, but Martinez had come only because it was convenient. He had fought the day before in the week-long *feria* at the Aguascalientes festival and it fit his schedule to make the short run over to the frontier for this meaningless *corrida*.

But it was not meaningless to Armillita and he spent a long time studying the five bulls they were to fight at five o'clock that afternoon. The animals were all together in the plank corral adjoining the dusty bullring. That, in itself, was a bad sign. If they were of any temperament, they should have been separated. They were from the Golderinas ranch and did not look particularly good. They were advertised as averaging nearly nine hundred pounds, but Armillita doubted that, just as he doubted that they'd cost $800 each as the promoter claimed. He leaned against the fence and watched them. Around him was an excited group of aficionados and ring employees and hangers-on. They showed him a deference he would not get from the average fan and were careful to make no motion or sound that might unduly excite the bulls.

Four of the bulls stood quietly, but one, a gray with an off-angled left horn, faced the corral fence and pawed and snorted at the people watching him. Armillita hoped he would not draw the animal for such bulls are notorious cowards and a cowardly bull is by far the worst in the ring.

It did not bother Armillita to be the only matador at the *sorteo* ceremony. He was used to it. Manolo's manager was there and a representative of Gaston Santos. The number of each bull was put in a hat and Santos's man drew one since the sportsman would fight only one animal. Then a discussion began between Armillita and Manolo's manager over the pairing of the four remaining bulls. This was done with much agitation even though each knew they were working blindly; there was no way to tell anything about such bulls until they came charging into the ring. Finally, after the animals had been discussed and their possible merits weighed, the pairings were agreed on. The gray bull was coupled with a medium-sized black that looked as good as any.

After the numbers of the bulls were written down, each participant had a hand in folding the small pieces of paper. Armillita did his part rather desultorily, but the manager rolled each into a tight ball, shifting them several times from hand to hand as if practicing a coin trick. Armillita thought the procedure overdone since none of the bulls were any damn good.

The drawing completed, he saw he had picked the gray. He immediately decided to fight the other bull first, the average-looking black, in hopes he might win the crowd early so that it would forgive him for what would probably happen with the gray. He knew these border crowds well. Since most of the spectators were poor they demanded a great deal for their money. And since they very seldom received it, they were quick to stand up and wave their ticket stubs and claim they had been cheated. Armillita didn't blame them, he just dreaded being the object of their derision. He would say, later in the afternoon, "It's true that the bulls here are very bad. But the crowds are worse."

He went back to the hotel and put on a pair of bathing trunks and lay down on the bed. He had left his door open and passing strangers would stop, look in, and say, "*Buena suerte,* good luck, matador." He was a tall, slim man of thirty two who didn't look very Mexican with his light skin and copper hair, but that was the Spanish influence in his background. Lying there on the bed he showed the results of several gorings. The horn goes ripping and tearing in and even the best surgeon cannot repair wounds without leaving heavy, ridged scar tissue. Armillita had four; a bad one in his left shoulder, one in his side, one in his thigh, and an unimpressive one in his lower leg. He had never had a femoral, a goring in the inside of the thigh that destroys the femoral artery. A matador can bleed to death from that before being carried from the ring.

His real name was Manuel Espinosa. He was called Armillita because his father had been called Armillita. The difference was that his father had been considered one of Mexico's best bullfighters. By now the son knew he would never approach his father's reputation.

A friend had come to act as Armillita's sword handler and equipment manager and to drive him to the ring. He got up and they embraced. The friend asked how he felt and how the bulls were; he shrugged and made a face. His friend said he had heard tickets were selling well and a good crowd was expected. The bullring held five thousand. Armillita shrugged and said that news was more important to Manolo Martinez than to him since Manola got a percentage of the gate while he got a fixed fee. He would receive about $2,000 for the fight, which sounded like a lot except he had to pay his *cuadrilla*—two *banderilleros* and one picador—out of that, as well as their traveling expenses, and his own expenses.

His *cuadrilla* were somewhere else in the hotel. They had driven down from Mexico City while he had flown. At four o'clock Chato, the old *banderillero* who had been with him for years, would come to help with the dressing ceremony. But that was a long time away, at least two hours, and he lay down to relax. He was hungry, but he was used to being hungry on Sunday afternoons. A bullfighter did not eat before a *corrida* because he might have to go under the surgeon's anesthesia. Another worry in these border fights was the lack of a good doctor. There were plenty in Mexico City and a good infirmary right in the Plaza de Toros. Here there was none of that and, if a matador got a bad horn wound, he just had to hope they could hold him together long enough to get him to the capital.

This was to be his last fight for a couple of months. He and his wife were going on a vacation to Germany. He was always nervous about a fight that was to be his last for a while. If you had a succession of fights ahead of you, there was no use fearing the one at hand for who knew what lay down the line. But here the tendency was strong to think, well, if I get through this one I'll be all right for a stretch of time.

In a corner of the room were boxes of Pampers, the disposable baby diapers. A visitor might think that these were of some use to the bullfighter, for stanching a wound or padding. But, no, their use was strictly as intended. They were cheaper on the United States side and Armillita's wife always asked him to pick up a supply when he was fighting on the border. She never went to his fights. He said, "Sweethearts like very much for you to be a matador. Wives never do. You are no longer the brave, glamorous bull-fighter then; you are a husband."

He had been a bullfighter for many years, beginning in his teens under the tutelage of his father and practicing on cows at their ranch. Since then he estimated he had killed somewhere around 1,200 bulls. He had fought all over, in Mexico, Spain, France, South America. There were not many years remaining, he expected, even with good luck—which was something a bullfighter had to count on.

At a few minutes to four Chato came and shooed the visitors out of the small room. Armillita went to the bathroom and showered and washed his hair. Then he returned and sat on the bed and cleaned his fingernails. He was meticulous about being completely clean when he went into the ring.

The dressing began with him sitting on the side of the bed with a towel wrapped around his middle. First came the long white undersocks. They were silk and required a lot of smoothing before they were exactly right. He secured them over his knees with elastic bands. Next he shucked the towel and pulled on the white linen pantaloons, the style of which is almost as old as the bullfight itself. These tied at the knees with strings. Next came the pink outer stockings, also silk. Except for the pants, which contained stretch material, the suit of lights remained traditional in style and fabric. But even with the stretch material, the pants were not easy to put on properly; it was a difficult job. To get them fitted in the crotch a rolled-up towel was used. Armillita held one end and Chato the other. The bullfighter straddled the towel and they both tugged and pulled. The pants in particular had to be skintight. A bullfighter wanted nothing loose that a horn might accidentally catch. Many people thought the pants needed to be tight in order to plainly show the bullfighter's *cojones*, but this was something dreamed up by tourists.

Next came the ruffled shirt and then the sash wrapped snugly around the waist. Then the thin tie and the vest of the heavy, brocaded jacket. This was pulled tight by inner snaps and Armillita had to hold his breath like a woman getting into a corset before Chato could arrange the fastenings.

Finally the shoes, like ballet slippers, and the black hat with lead in it, and they were ready to go. The friend had carried down the equipment, the swords and capes and muletas, and put them in the truck of the car. Armillita paused to say a prayer in front of his portable chapel, going to his knees awkwardly in the tight pants. Chato stood just behind the matador, praying too. Then Armillita made the sign of the cross, kissed his thumb, and they left.

Piedras Negras was very hot and Armillita began sweating almost immediately. The car did not have air conditioning and it was hotter still on the road to the bullring. The suit of lights weighed a little more than twelve pounds. It had cost about $600 and he would use it, barring accidents, for a dozen *corridas*. Special-class matadors paid more for theirs and used them for only six or eight fights. When he had to buy a new one Armillita would sell his old suit to a *banderillero* or novice bullfighter for one or two hundred dollars.

As they neared the ring there was the usual group of urchins and young men at the entrance. They crowded around the car, peering in the window to see the matador. Several officious police could do little to help as the car inched into the parking lot.

The ring was of drab-white concrete rising suddenly on the plain just at the edge of town. Structural steel sticking out here and there gave it an unfinished air. The ring was so small it did not have the required chapel in which the matadors could pray just before the *paseo*. All bullfighters are strict Catholics. Armillita's friend, who had been an interested *novillero* before he foolishly tried to kill a bull in his *querencia* (the section of the ring where the animal feels most secure), said, "There is a comfort in the ritual, as if a man has satisfied himself he's done all he can for his own protection."

Bullfights begin with very little preparation. There is no way for matadors to warm up, so they arrive just before the performance and then wait in the tunnel to make their formal entrance. Manolo Martinez was already there and Armillita greeted him with an embrace. Manolo looked tired and drawn around the eyes. He had driven that morning from Aguascalientes and then spent the afternoon sleeping in the hotel. He didn't look very interested in the proceedings. He had been drunk at nine that morning, having celebrated with his friends and followers.

It was even hotter in the tunnel, but suddenly they were opening the gate and the band was striking up and the three men were proceeding across the loose sand of the arena. Armillita looked up, seeing the full stands. He hoped the crowd contained a goodly share of American tourists. They never cared what they saw. All they wanted was to drink beer and yell and laugh and have a good time.

The matadors walked to the barrier on the far side from the entrance of the bulls and laid their ceremonial capes over the wall. All around them attendants bustled. Gaston Santos would fight first, then Manolo would have his first bull, then Armillita, then Manolo again and then Armillita would end it with the gray. But none would be through until the finish, for a bullfighter, by law, must aid the other matadors on the card, if necessary. The promoter is responsible under the law for the size and breeding of the bulls he has advertised. If they are not up to specifications he can be fined or jailed, though in Piedras Negras no one remembered the last time such a thing had happened.

While Santos was performing his equestrian ballet against his bull, Manolo and Armillita stood behind the barrier discussing conditions. Manolo said the wind was terrible, as, indeed, it was. A stray gust can blow the cape or *muleta* back against the body and the bull with his horns follows. To combat this, the *peones* wet the bottom of the fighting capes and scuff them in the sand to make them heavier. But a cape cannot be too heavy or else the bullfighter's wrist numbs and he loses the fine touch he needs to control the bull.

Armillita was particularly concerned about the sand. "It's too loose," he said. "The bulls will be slipping all over."

"Oh yes," Manolo said, "the bulls, such as they are." He laughed. He was not particularly concerned about conditions or the bulls. He had flatly announced back in his hotel room that he was not going to overwork. He had explained, "It is pointless to attempt anything here. If you did the fans would not understand."

Santos killed his bull, which the crowd liked well enough, and Manolo moved out into the ring while his *peones* spread their capes before the early charges of his first bull. Armillita stood behind the barrier and watched, thinking how he would fight Manolo's bull.

Manolo, as he had said he would, fought safely. He risked nothing, and the fans, sensing this, began to resent it even before he was half through. Watching, Armillita knew he was going to inherit some of this enmity. Still, he admired the technical skills that Manolo was displaying, even when he went in to kill in such a fashion that he exposed very little of himself. That, too, took skill, even if it was a talent employed to deceive the crowd. But the crowd was not going to be duped. The price of the bullfight represented a day's pay to many of the spectators and they were getting hot. Armillita listened to their outrage and merely shrugged and smiled when asked what he thought. "I believe," he said, "they will understand there are some bulls with which nothing can be done."

His first was not that way, however. He was not a great bull or even a good one, but he appeared, when he came skidding into the ring, to be a bull a man could put on a show with. Armillita went out with the cape, walking with an awkward long-legged stride, while his *peones* worked the bull toward him. He took the animal through a series of simple passes, nothing extravagant or showy, and then chopped him off short while the crowd settled back. The bull was working straight and honest and so was Armillita. A fan in the first barrier seats said, "At least Armillita won't cheat you. He'll give you his best."

The trumpets blew and the picadors came into the ring and Armillita picked up the bull and presented him to the first horse. It was going well. The bull charged readily, thudding its horns futilely but determinedly into the mattress padding protecting the horse's belly. The bull kept boring in, stronger and stronger, as the picador shot his lance into the big hump of muscle just behind the neck. Armillita went in, made the *quite*, and then decided, since the bull still seemed too strong, to take it to the second picador for more trimming. But that was a mistake. The second picador was too zealous and the spectators were starting to boo even as he leaned into his lance. They could see he was bearing down too hard, giving the bull too much steel, hurting it too badly, and fearing the bull would be ruined, they were reacting violently. Armillita went in and tried valiantly to perform the *quite*, but the bull would not move away from the horse and the picador could not remove his lance or else the bull would have thrown him. By the time Armillita could distract the bull the damage was done and the crowd had turned permanently ill-humored.

He killed the bull moderately well, but it made no difference to the spectators. They believed the animal had been rendered harmless by the picador and that any of them could have done as well as the matador. Armillita walked back to the barrier, head down, not bothering to ask for an ear or even a circuit of the ring as he might well have done.

Manolo was no better with his second bull than his first and it was necessary, before Armillita's last bull was released, for two attendants to parade around with a sign saying anyone throwing anything into the ring would be fined 500 pesos. But it did no good. Manolo, because of his exalted position, had been received with sullen silence. But Armillita was none too good even for such a bullring, and as soon as his picadors entered the ring the cushions and bottles came flying. Though these were not intended for Armillita, a bottle nearly hit him as he went to take the bull away from the first picador. This time he did not present the bull to the second picador, but instead asked for their retirement. The crowd cheered that cynically, and he faced the spectators and smiled and lifted his arms as if to say, "My friends, what else can I do?"

The gray bull was all he'd expected, stodgy and slow and reluctant to make more than a head-chopping charge of a few steps. And then, midway through the planting of the *banderillas*, it took up a *querencia* only a few feet from the barrier. This made the planting of the last set a difficult proposition and gave the crowd a chance to attack Armillita's second *banderillero* who, because the bull would not move, ended up planting them a third of the way down the animal's side. Again bottles and cushions cascaded into the ring.

Armillita tried to move the bull with the *muleta,* but it was reluctant. The animal would charge a few steps when the matador incited it with his knee, but then quickly retreat before any semblance of a linked pass could be put together.

Finally Armillita gave up. He asked and received permission to kill the bull and then walked to the center of the ring and, in a gesture either sardonic or placating, offered to dedicate the bull to the crowd. Smiling all the while, he held up his *montera* and spun slowly on his heel through a full circle offering the spectators the bull. But they wouldn't have it. They yelled and jeered and waved handkerchiefs and some began to leave. Finally he shrugged and walked back to the barrier for a drink of water. His mouth was very dry, as it always was in the ring.

Manolo was sympathetic. "What can you do with such people?" he said. "Don't let them bother you. Slaughter that ox and let's get the hell out of here." Armillita wanted to say, "These are the people whom I usually fight for." But he didn't.

The bull was difficult to kill. This was partly because of the kind of animal it was, but mainly because it had taken a very determined *querencia.* Armillita could not move the bull to get its feet lined up so that the spot between the shoulder blades would be open. Each time Armillita would go in with the sword, the bull would chop upward with its head, paying little attention to the muleta in the matador's left hand. Armillita tried twice, taking considerable risks each time. Each time the sword only penetrated a few inches, to be flipped out by the bull's muscles. Finally he went to the barrier and took the *descabellar* from his volunteer sword handler. "You should have used this in the first place," his friend said. "No one can blame you for this bull. Kill it any way you can."

The crowd booed the *descabellar*, a strong daggerlike sword that the matador plunges into the spinal cord just behind the head. It is an ungraceful way to kill but sometimes the only way. But even as Armillita maneuvered the bull into position and leaped forward to perform the final act the cushions and bottles were coming down again. There were not so many this time, but that may have been because ammunition was getting low in the stands.

Then it was over and the mules were dragging out the gray. Armillita went over to the barrier and took a long drink of water and sagged down tiredly. His friend was busy packing the equipment and the plaza was emptying rapidly. Manolo stopped by for a moment and said he would see Armillita back at the hotel. Armillita just nodded. After a time he gathered up his ceremonial cape and walked to the car where his friend was waiting.

That evening Manolo's suite was jammed with fifteen or twenty of his friends and employees. Some newspaper people were trying to interview him, but this was almost impossible because of the enthusiastic help of his friends who kept trying to tell the reporters how great Manolo was. He was finally asked about the bullfight while lying on the bed drinking Scotch, with just a towel over his middle. He said, "What? Oh, this was nothing. This wasn't a bullfight."

Armillita's room was not packed with well-wishers. His friend had gone. After showering he called his wife, then his mother, then the newspapers in Mexico City. This was a ritual he followed after every fight. To his wife and mother he said little more than he was all right, but to the newspapers he gave a stylized version of the fight that included none of the bad parts. He knew that Manolo's press agent would be doing the same thing so he told the story without fear of contradiction. It was not a duty a matador ought to perform, but it was part of his life. Later Chato came in and Armillita took out a roll of peso notes and paid off his *cuadrilla*. There was a brief argument over an expense item, but in the end Armillita let it go.

He lay down on the bed. Then he got up again. He had heard

there might be a change on the card at an important *corrida* in Juarez that was coming up soon and he wanted to put in his bid. If he could fight there he might put off his vacation. In the end, however, he decided it was too late to call the promoter. He lay down again and yawned. Then he turned on the TV. It was too early to go to sleep.

18

Ring of Truth

I didn't much want to do this story in the first place. I was in the midst of trying to get divorced from my second wife and the idea of going down to the border to see a novice bullfighter just didn't appeal to me.

But I went. The only part I enjoyed was the photographer, Tomas Pantin from Venezuela. Normally I don't get along with photographers on a job. They turn that motor drive on and click off nine million shots and think they've created some form of art. Then they send in a stack of proof sheets and the art director picks one or two shots out of the multitude he's been furnished and all of a sudden this guy has created something. Hell, with those kind of odds a monkey has got to end up with a few good shots.

I used to be famous for firing photographers. The magazine would assign them to a story that was my idea in the first place and they'd show up acting like they owned the action. They'd say, with all those cameras hanging off their neck, "What's the story going to be about?"

And I'd say, "How the hell do I know? I just got here myself."

Some of them thought they were running the story. Right up until the time I'd have them call the magazine and find out that, yes, I could fire them.

I still can't stand photographers, but Tomas Pantin was a little different. About the second day we were in Piedras Negras I went to grousing around and said I couldn't drink the Mexican beer, that it was too heavy, and if I didn't get some light beer I was leaving. No writer, no story. No story, no need for a photographer.

So that evening Tomas drove across the border and brought me back a case of Miller Lite beer. He said he did it out of concern and friendship.

I think he did it because he was getting $500 a day and the story was about a five-day job.

This was what Paco Olivera had waited eight years for. Tomorrow he was to take his *alternativa* at the bullfight, tomorrow he would cease being a *novillero,* a novice, and join that select group of bullfighters who have mastered their profession and become matadors. Even the word was like a tonic to him; his face would light up each time he found occasion to pronounce it, savoring the stately Spanish cadence that draws the word out into three distinct syllables: "*ma-ta-dor.*" He had been waiting for this night since he was twelve, when he had announced his intention of becoming a matador. Now that it had come, his pride knew no bounds.

At twenty, Paco is small and, like all bullfighters, extremely graceful. He was sitting at the head of a long table in the brightly lit cafe in Reynosa, flanked by the members of his *cuadrilla,* the team that assisted him in the bullring. His manager was there, as was his *mozo,* the personal servant who would act as his sword handler and attend him during the dressing ceremony the next day. There were also several of his *novillero* friends who had driven up from Mexico City to be with him for this important occasion. They could not quite hide their envy.

Nor could the other patrons of the cafe resist glancing over at the young man sitting so nonchalantly in his chair. Perhaps they did not know who he was, but there is something in the way a bullfighter carries himself, even in the way he holds his head and moves his hands, that announces his identity to the world. Bullfighters are different from American athletes. They are held in a special awe that transcends their ability or their courage. Even the mediocre ones are considered to be in a class above normal mortals, are regarded as a kind of combination of priest and athlete.

Paco was very conscious of this, conscious that this was his time and his alone. It was not important that his *alternativa* was being taken in an insignificant plaza in the border town of Reynosa rather than in the Plaza México in Mexico City. A plaza such as Reynosa's does not draw the true aficionados, and the matadors do not put out their best, for they know the fans will not notice, much less appreciate, the finer points of their art. But none of that mattered to Paco. What did matter was that he would be given his initiation by Manolo Martinez, the number one matador in all the world.

Paco had worked hard for the honor. If you were to go down to the Plaza México in the early morning you would see perhaps five hundred would-be *novilleros*, some as young as ten years of age, working out with their capes just as Paco had. Some would be charging each other, their hands at the sides of their heads to simulate horns; some would be caping the trundle, a two-wheeled cart with a set of horns mounted on its front; some would be working alone, others under the tutelage of retired *banderilleros* or matadors. Of the five hundred you would see on any given morning, perhaps four or five would actually get the chance to fight a bull as a *novillero*. And of these, the odds were very good that none would become a full matador.

Paco had fought as a novice since he was sixteen and had killed over a hundred bulls in sixty-eight *corridas*. Cynics might say that Paco's rich family had paid Manolo to preside at his *alternativa*, but Manolo was already about as rich as a bullfighter can get. Besides, it is not good politics for a senior matador to put his stamp of approval on a *novillero* who will turn out to be nothing. That sort of thing is remembered in bullfighting. Manolo was there because he thought the young *novillero* had promise.

To make the honor greater still, the number three matador, Antonio Lomelín, would also be appearing on the card. For many aficionados, this was the real draw; since Antonio does not have the technical skills of Manolo, he takes more risks. He is also a more emotional killer when he goes in over the horns.

But as Paco celebrated in the cafe, neither of the matadors was yet in town. They would not arrive until the next day. Paco, of course, had come in early. In fact, he had already been down to look at the bulls. Leaning over the heavy corral fence, he'd studied the six sleek fighting machines, these arbiters of his destiny. The bulls had been advertised at 475 kilos, or a little over 1,000 pounds, each. Under Mexican law, bulls under 450 kilos may not be fought in a corrida by full matadors. An impresario who puts on a *corrida* with bulls under 450 kilos or under the age of four years can be fined or sent to prison. But such an occurrence is beyond the memory of anyone. And certainly the bulls slated for Paco's *alternativa* seemed of the proper age and weight. He surveyed them all closely but would not say which he preferred to draw. "No," he said, "for me that is bad luck."

At the table that evening an American tourist who had heard

that Paco was a matador came over to talk bullfighting. It was the tourist's first bullfight. He asked Paco if he didn't feel sorry for the bull. The *novillero* regarded him with surprise. "No," he said, "of course not. Does he feel the sympathy for me?" One felt love, respect, affection for a good bull, he explained, but never pity or sympathy. But the man didn't understand how he could love the bull and then kill him. How did Paco feel when the bull was dead? he pressed. Paco smiled, his white teeth gleaming. "*Contento,*" he replied.

He was becoming tired of the man, so he didn't try to explain the *corrida* further. He knew it was useless: you can't make someone understand who does not feel it inside. Bullfighting, to Paco, is making art, and art made in the face of death is great art. But he knows that others see only the blood and the suffering of the bull. They think it quite all right for a steer to be hit in the head with a sledgehammer, but they consider it cruel for a fighting bull to be killed with a sword.

Most Anglos find it difficult to appreciate the meaning of the bullfight because they think of it as a celebration of death, rather than what it is — a defiance of death. According to the Spanish mystique, the bullfighter is the spectator's surrogate against death. If he enters the arena of his own volition and faces death willingly, then can death be such a terrible enemy? To maintain this illusion, it is very important that the matador face the possibility of destruction with superb grace and disdain. He must work close to the horns; he must take risks. Otherwise there is no point. A cowardly matador who uses tricks and gimmicks and stays well clear of the bull's horns incites the crowd's anger; he has defeated the very purpose of the *corrida de toros.*

But one does not say these things to matadors, or to *novilleros* who are about to become matadors. They may understand them inside, but they don't speak of them. Such talk is reserved for philosophers and intense aficionados who feel a need to explain the *fiesta brava* in terms *they* can understand.

Certainly no such weighty constructs clouded Paco's mind as he left the cafe to walk to his hotel room. The only thing he said was directed to his manager. "If I get bull seventy-one [which he had privately decided was the best of the six], should I fight him for my *alternativa* or save him for last for the crowd?" he asked.

His manager answered, "Let us wait until we get bull seventy-one to decide."

As they parted Paco joked, "Now the only thing that can stop me from becoming a matador is if I'm killed in a car wreck on the way to the plaza." And that was true. For he would take his *alternativa* in the ring before he fought his first bull; even if that bull killed him, he would still die a matador.

Paco slept late the next morning, staying in bed until it was almost time to go to the *sorteo*, the pairing and drawing of the bulls. It would not take place until twelve-thirty, but Antonio Lomelín, who had arrived that morning, went an hour earlier to look over the bulls. The corral was already swarming with factotums and aficionados. Making his way through the crowd, Antonio was waylaid many times to sign autographs, to talk, or just to exchange greetings. When he finally reached the corral he studied the bulls for a long time. Photographers from the Mexican papers surrounded him, cameras clicking. Antonio is a handsome man, somewhat larger than Paco, but his face shows the strain and fatigue of the sixty to seventy *corridas* he fights each year.

As the matador watched, his manager threw rocks at the bulls to make them move around so Antonio could study how they carried their heads and thus learn which horn they might favor. (A bull is either left-horned or right-horned, meaning he prefers to hook with that horn. The matador, naturally, will always want to pass him on the other horn.) Antonio had liked bulls 71 and 63, just as Paco had.

The *sorteo* is a very important part of the *corrida*. Generally, there are six bulls and three bullfighters, so each matador will fight two bulls. A manager would like to see the two best bulls paired so that his matador will have a chance to draw the two best fighting bulls in the *corrida*. Instead, as a compromise, the managers usually agree to pair the bulls in a best-worst coupling.

The ceremony for assigning the bulls to the matadors has not changed for perhaps a hundred years. A disinterested party takes three cigarettes, empties the tobacco from them, and writes a pair of numbers on each of the papers. Then the managers roll the papers into very hard little balls. The balls are put in a hat and each manager draws for his matador. The president of the bullring stands by to record which bulls each fighter has drawn. Very solemnly he receives the cigarette papers and transfers the bulls' numbers to the official ledger.

Antonio did not stay for the *sorteo*; it was beneath his dignity to do so. But Paco was there. He drew bull 71, which had been coupled with bull 37. He and his manager decided that he would fight bull 71 for his *alternativa* and then do the best he could with bull 37 later.

"I must please the people," he said. "And I think this is the best way."

Paco was happy with the draw. Both of his bulls were *corniabiertos*, open-horned bulls that are less likely to give the matador a *cornada*, a goring. The other four bulls were *cerrados*, bulls whose horns point forward, allowing them to inflict more serious injuries. Antonio Lomelín has had sixteen femorals, wounds to the inside of the thigh that pierce the femoral artery. These are the most dangerous wounds in bullfighting—without immediate medical attention a matador can bleed to death in minutes. Antonio has been lucky: all his femorals have occurred in important bullrings that were equipped with an infirmary, where a surgeon was standing by. But there was neither infirmary nor surgeon at the arena at Reynosa.

At five o'clock, in his hotel room, Paco proceeded with the lengthy dressing ceremony. His *mozo,* Jorge López, had come in to assist him. Paco was nervous. He held his right hand out to judge the degree to which he was shaking. There was a certain tremble, but he was far steadier than one would have imagined under the circumstances.

By the time he finished, a small crowd was standing against the far wall. Paco's manager was there, as well as his father and grandfather and a number of the *novilleros*. But Paco paid no attention to them; it was plain that his mind had turned inward to the two bulls he would face that evening. His *mozo* helped him on with the ruffled shirt, then wrapped the sash snugly around his waist. Next came the thin tie and the heavy brocaded vest and jacket. The *mozo* pulled the vest tight and fastened its inner snaps. Paco had to hold his breath like a woman getting into a corset before his servant could make the fastenings come together. After that came the shoes, like ballet slippers, and the black hat, the *montera*, with lead in it to make it stay securely on his head. The last act was the tying of the tassled strings called *machos* at the knees of his pants.

Paco was ready. His "suit of lights," which had been bought by his father for this very special occasion, had cost $900. Normally a bullfighter pays around $600 for a *traje de luces*. He will wear it, barring mishaps, for six to eight fights and then sell it to a *banderillero* or a *novillero* for a couple of hundred dollars. But Paco was not going to sell his suit. It would go into a glass case in the parlor of his father's house in Mexico City.

The *mozo* and the *peones*, as the *banderilleros* are called, collected Paco's sword case, *muleta* (the small killing cape), and fighting cape. His father held the door open for him, and the procession descended the stairs, Paco walking very proudly. His third cape, the ceremonial one, was wrapped around his left arm. In the lobby and in the parking lot several women rushed up to kiss him on the cheek and to wish him good luck. He accepted the affection stiffly, for his mind was now on the bulls. But the kisses were very much a part of the tradition.

In the car Paco was very quiet. A crowd awaited him as he pulled into the back of the arena. Several officious policemen were on hand, but they were ineffective against the throng of people who swarmed toward the suit of lights. With the help of his entourage Paco struggled through the gate to the alleyway that led to the door from which he would make the *paseo*, his entrance. Antonio and Manolo were already there, their ceremonial capes hung over their right arms. They were laughing and joking with each other and with the aficionados who surrounded them. But they stopped when Paco came up and gave them a formal bow. In turn they each gave him an *abrazo*, a hug, which in Mexico is much more meaningful than a handshake.

It was now only moments before the grand entrance. Paco went to the little private chapel and knelt before the Virgin. In his room he had prayed for ten minutes in front of his own portable chapel while his entourage stood silent and respectful. Now he was saying another prayer, bending awkwardly in his suit of lights. When he had finished he rejoined Antonio and Manolo, who stood stiffly in front of the gate. Paco was in blue with gold trim, Antonio was in red, and Manolo was dressed from head to toe in gold. Only a matador can wear gold. If a *banderillero* buys an old suit of lights from a matador he must remove the gold braid.

Outside in the *callejón*, the space between the barrier and the stands, the impresario, Luis Tamez, stood looking up at the crowd. He was anxious—it appeared that he was about to lose money. There were perhaps five thousand seats, of which three thousand were now filled. At $7 a person, that made his take around $21,000.

The six bulls had cost $9,000; Manolo had cost $7,000 and Antonio $6,000. If there were enough left over Tamez would have to pay Paco $1,000. But that was highly unlikely. At best, the impresario would break even.

Despite its popularity, the *corrida de toros* makes few men wealthy. At one time bullfighting served the same function in Mexico that boxing did in the United States: it was a way for a poor boy to get out of the slums. But no longer. Now the *novillero's* family must have money to pay for practice bulls and assistants. For four years Paco's father, who is a rich architect in Mexico City, and his grandfather had paid for his passion. Still, Paco's chances of earning the kind of money that Manolo and Antonio make are very slim indeed.

As the trumpets sounded, the attendants swung open the gates for the matadors. The trio came walking across the sand of the arena, Manolo Martinez in the middle, Antonio on his right, and Paco, as was proper, walking one step back. Behind the bullfighters strode their *cuadrillas*. The crowd cheered as they crossed the arena, and the matadors raised their arms in acknowledgment.

All except Paco. By now he was very pale. He came to the barrier and accepted the fighting cape from his *mozo*. "*Agua*," he said in a tight voice, holding out the cape so that water could be poured on it. Then he scuffed it in the sand to make the bottom heavier.

The trumpets blew and the first bull came skidding into the arena. Paco stood behind the barrier and studied the animal while his *banderilleros* took it through a series of passes. He was watching to see which horn the bull favored, to see how easily he was incited to charge. Paco watched for perhaps two minutes and then walked out into the arena, waving away the *banderilleros*, adjusting his cape, walking toward bull 71. He took the bull through one pass, the classic veronica that looks so simple, yet requires such skill. Then he motioned to the *banderilleros* to take the bull away and walked back to the barrier. Manolo came out to meet him. They embraced. It was the moment Paco had waited years for. Manolo said, "Now you are a matador. And I welcome you."

"Thank you, maestro," Paco replied. Then Antonio came out and embraced him. Across the arena the *banderilleros* were keeping the bull occupied, but no one was paying any attention to them. The senior matadors retired. Paco lifted his *montera* and, holding it aloft, slowly turned a circle to acknowledge the applause. But he did not dedicate the bull to the crowd. He had reserved that honor for the man who had made this moment possible. His father was sitting in the front row; Paco walked to the edge and pitched his *montera* to him. Then his father leaned over the high wall and they embraced. The crowd cheered its appreciation of the gesture.

Paco had been mistaken about bull 71. He was not a good bull; he was cowardly and would not charge. Paco did the best he could with the cape, but he could not put together a series of linked passes. The bull would do nothing but make little chopping rushes and then stand panting, staring at Paco. At one point the new matador walked up and slapped the beast on the muzzle — with no effect.

Finally Paco summoned the mounted picadors to shoot the iron point of the lance into the bull's hump. This is done to make his head come down so that the matador can go in with his sword over the horns. Most matadors are so short and the bulls so tall that if the tossing muscle is not weakened the matador has no chance. But Paco allowed only one blow and a very mild one at that. Then he performed the *quite,* the use of the cape to take the bull away from the horse.

The trumpets blew for the *banderillas,* the barbed darts that are thrust into the bull's shoulders. Many people think they are for goading the bull, but that is not true. They are used to correct his hooking tendencies. If a bull hooks with his right horn, the *banderillero* places the barbs on the left side to make him more conscious of that side so that he will charge straight ahead. This timid bull required no correction, and the placing of the *banderillas* was an emotionless event.

Paco began trying to work the bull into a kill position. He had taken the *muleta* and sword from his *mozo.* The bull would not charge. Paco incited him with the *muleta,* stamping his foot, but it was no use. The bull had taken up a position against the barrier in his *querencia,* his turf, and he refused to come out. This is the most dangerous place in the ring to try to kill a bull, for he can simply stand still and hook both ways as the matador comes in over the horns. Manolo, watching from behind the barrier, shouted, "No, make him come away."

But Paco did not seem to hear him. He walked toward the bull. His face was very pale. The bull just stood there. Paco tried to get him to charge the *muleta,* but he refused. He stood with his feet spread, a posture that closes the shoulder blades so the sword will not go in. A bullfighter tries to position the bull so that his front feet are close together. That opens the killing spot, which, at most, is only as big as a half-dollar. It is obviously very difficult, even under the best circumstances, to go in over the horns, looking down a three-foot sword, and hit that tiny spot.

Manolo yelled again, "No!" But still Paco would not hear him. He profiled, incited the bull with the cape, and plunged in over the horns. The sword went in a quarter of the way, then flipped out. A *banderillero* retrieved it and handed it to Paco, who was sweating and ashen. He walked back to the barrier to rinse his mouth out. He looked up at his father, who could only spread his hands in a gesture of resignation.

Five times Paco went in over the horns, with no opportunity to make the kill with grace and nobility. The bull would do nothing but stand chopping sideways with his horns. In the end Paco simply gathered himself up and, disregarding the danger, went at the bull in such a way that the sword could not miss. It was a very dangerous kill, but it was effective.

Paco came back to the barrier drenched in sweat. Antonio tried to console him. "You did well with that basket of bones. The best surgeon in Mexico could not have gotten a scalpel in him."

But that was not the way Paco had wanted it to be. Every *novillero* wants to be awarded an ear on his *alternativa*, just as every rookie in the major leagues wants to hit a home run his first time at the plate. The crowd had been sympathetic to his situation, but they were not about to demean the sport by awarding him a trophy for his less than exciting effort. His had been a bad bull, but it is, after all, the job of a matador to make a good bull out of a bad one. And Paco had not done that.

Manolo, in a very nice gesture, dedicated his first bull to Paco. In an amazing feat of technical skill, he ran his sword in and out of the bull three times before he finally killed him. He did it to show his contempt for the quality of the bulls. Before he made the final thrust he gave the president of the bullring a mock salute with his sword, as if to say, "Do you expect a bullfighter of my stature to fight such bulls? You should not have let the fight go on." It was also his way of telling the crowd, "This young man, who is today becoming a full matador, deserves a better chance with better bulls. I, Manolo Martinez, the number one bullfighter in all the world, can tell you so."

Then Antonio fought his first bull, received the ear, and was roundly applauded by the crowd. Manolo did a technician's job on his last bull and retired, yawning, to the barrier. Antonio was awarded another ear on a bad bull that he corrected, and then it was Paco's last chance.

When the bull came into the arena Paco met him sliding on his knees to do the pass of death. Bull 37 turned out to be the best of the day, but even with a good animal Paco could not achieve the style of Manolo Martinez or Antonio Lomelín. In the end he killed the bull with adequate grace, and the crowd waved handkerchiefs to ask the president of the bullring to give him an ear. One of his *banderilleros* cut off the ear and Paco paraded around the ring with it while the ladies in the crowd threw roses and purses and the men threw wineskins. Paco gathered the roses up in his left arm, still holding the ear in his right hand. His *banderilleros* threw the purses back to the crowd and Paco picked up the wineskins and used the wine to wash off his face. He did not drink because he, like all bullfighters, drinks very little, if at all.

In the end he stood facing the president of the bullring, still carrying the roses, and held the bull's ear aloft in a supplicating gesture. The president did not award him the ear. The crowd wanted him to have it, but the president as much as said to him, "Now you are a matador, and you must earn an ear the same as any other matador."

That night Paco went to the hotel where Manolo and Antonio had stayed. They were checking out to go to their next bullfight. He embraced them both formally and thanked them. He looked very young in his slacks and sports shirt, and they looked very old in theirs. "I have realized this night," he told them, "that now I must be in competition with Antonio Lomelín and Manolo Martinez. I must please the crowd the same. I will no longer be treated as a boy, as a novice. It will be difficult, I think."

A little later Antonio sat in the restaurant. As he waited to be driven to the airport he was asked why he had chosen to become a matador, a question for which there are probably as many answers as there are bullfighters. Paco, confronted earlier with that question, had said, "For the honor of my family." But

Antonio's answer cut to the heart of the matter. He said simply, "Because it is part of my spirit."

Asked how Paco had done, he laughed. "Well, he made a lot of mistakes. But what else is to be expected?" Then he became very serious. "The young man took his *alternativa*. That is nothing. The real *alternativa* is when you lie on the surgeon's table with the bad *cornada*, with the blood draining out of you, thinking, 'This is the last bull I will ever fight. And he killed me.' The young man has never had a true *cornada*. Let him lie on that table and make his prayer, 'God, please let me have one more bull to fight before I die.' Then he will be a matador."

19

The Bloody Sport
of Kite Fighting

*This one was a joy. Haven't you ever nad dreams of suddenly getting big
and strong and putting the school bully in his place? Well, this was about
what the whole deal amounted to and was just as satisfying.*

*I've been making flying kites all my life, but this was by far the most
enjoyable experience I'd ever had. Boy, did I whip that guy's ass.*

With a little help, you understand.

So you didn't think kite fighting was a major blood sport. Well,
neither did I until the time I was innocently flying one on the
beach at Corpus Christi, Texas. It was just coming dusk and
I wasn't doing much more than enjoying the sea breeze and the
setting sun and hoping nobody was snickering at a middle-aged
man flying a kite.

Well, about that time a man suddenly came up from behind me
flying an ominous-looking blue kite that he was showing remarkable control with, from a sort of rod and reel combination.

My kite was just one of those little Hi-Fliers, the kind made of
sticks and paper that you buy at the local convenience store. We
were on a vacation and I'd bought the kite on a whim, thinking it
would be a nice way to enjoy the beach and to try something I
hadn't done since I was a kid.

My newly arrived neighbor had taken a position about ten yards
to my right. I'd looked over at him and nodded and said something
about its being a nice evening, but all he'd done was give me a cold,
grim smile. Then he began making that kite of his stunt, swooping

and climbing and turning right and left. It was not the same configuration as my little diamond-shaped kite, but seemed to have a body and wings and a sort of spread-out tail like you'd see on a hawk. I didn't realize it at the moment, but the maneuvers he was putting his kite through were a sort of cat and mouse game. I was about to compliment him on his kite's performance when he suddenly swooped within ten feet of my little paper contraption.

That should have been my first warning of danger, but then I hadn't been smart enough to recognize the unfriendly expression on his face. The next thing I knew he'd made an even closer pass. I said, "Hey, watch it!" Looking around I saw he'd moved within about five yards of me. I moved down the beach a few steps thinking that perhaps he was having trouble with the wind.

He said, "That won't do you any good."

I still didn't know what was going on, but I was somewhat relieved when I noticed he'd let out enough line so that his kite was a good fifty feet above mine.

He said, "Kiss it goodbye." The next thing I knew that devil kite of his came swooping down on my little toy and hit it a stunning blow and then went sweeping away.

I yelled, "What the hell!"

I'd never seen a fighting kite before, and I'd certainly never been bullied by one. For a minute I was busy trying to reel my broken flying machine in. But it was a futile effort and the kite fell into the sea. I'd been yelling at him all the time as to just what the hell he thought he was doing, but, by the time I was able to turn around and look, he'd disappeared into the gathering night.

Well, that night at the hotel I did some brooding. I'm talking major-league brooding. I mean that man had assaulted an ex-rodeo cowboy, a bull rider! And not only that, but an ex-Junior College football player and a man who'd had a tryout with the St. Louis Cardinals.

I do not suffer humiliation lightly, so the next day I went down the Causeway and found a kite shop I'd noticed before. Apparently they fly a lot of kites on the beach, but I hadn't known it was in the same league with professional boxing and nineteenth-century dueling.

I'd never seen such a variety of kites as were in that shop. I told the man there behind the counter rather grimly and somewhat heatedly about what had happened. He wanted to know what the man and his kite had looked like. I told him about the kite and then said the man was slim and dark and looked to be in his early thirties.

The name of the man behind the counter turned out to be Jay Hall. He just said: "Oh, that would be Kenneth. That's his specialty. He's what we call a raider."

"A what?"

"A raider. He likes to find kites he knows he can beat just for practice. He gets his kicks out of it."

I said, "Build me a kite I can beat him with."

Jay shook his head. "I can build you a kite, but Kenneth is pretty good. You don't sound like you've had much experience. And fighting kites, especially one that would have a chance against him, cost a lot of money."

Sometimes words come out of my mouth that I don't mean to say, but I was in a reckless mood so I said, "I don't care. Cost is no object. And I'm hiring you as my coach. On the spot. I just want to knock that devil out of the sky and straight into the ocean."

Jay was a fair-haired young man with a chest that could make you seriously believe he was a weight lifter. He got a kind of thoughtful look in his eyes and said, "You serious?"

"Serious as rancid milk."

"He's good."

"I'm mean. And also vengeful."

"It'll take a lot of practice."

"There'll be no vacation for me until my honor has been satisfied." (I didn't really say that, but it sounds a lot better than what I did say.)

He said, "Okay. You got a deal. I've been wanting to get that so-and-so for some time. And you might just be the pigeon we can set him up with." Well, I didn't particularly care for that remark, but we struck a deal.

We finally settled on a design that was a sort of a flying wing that would be constructed out of fiberglass crossmembers and a mylar plastic covering. I had wanted the conventional diamond shape, but Jay had explained, "If we build it like that I'll have to put a long tail on it to maintain stability and that's the first thing Kenneth is going to attack. He's got razor blades all over that kite and, once he cuts your tail, you're gone. With this design I can put on a short stabilizing tail and use a sort of aluminum-coated material he can't cut. As it is we're giving up a lot of mobility to his kite, but I don't think that matters. I don't think there's time for you to learn to handle a kite like Kenneth. We'll have to outthink him."

Our kite came out with a wing span of five feet and ran a little over four feet nose to tail. Jay said, "I'm building a four-inch plastic ramming spike into the nose. That's what you got to get him with."

"I don't care if you mount a .50-caliber machine gun in the kite," I said, "so long as I have my finger on the trigger."

He said, "This kite is slightly bigger than his and somewhat heavier so you're going to have to learn to handle it. But what's worrying me is the bridle. I've got to figure out one that will give you the kind of control you'll need to get him at the precise second he's vulnerable."

I said, "Just coach and call the plays. Don't tell me the game plan."

We practiced. For three days we went out every evening to a deserted stretch of beach and worked with that kite. At first it reined under my inexperienced hands like a bucking horse. Jay would become exasperated and yell, "You're over-controlling! Gently, gently! That bridle is sensitive and so is that kite!"

I thought he was going to give up on me, but the day came when he said, "Okay, we're ready. Tomorrow is Saturday and that's Kenneth's favorite raiding day because all the kids and pigeons are flying on the beach. You go down and buy one of those Hi-Fliers and I'll meet you later."

Well, I started to protest, but he just said, "Do what I tell you. I'll be there with your kite at the right time."

Outside the condominium where my wife and I were staying was a long pier. It was adjacent to the very stretch of beach where Kenneth had shot me down. On Jay's instructions I went out and put my little paper kite up in the air while he stayed under the pier with the kite he had christened, quite inappropriately for my purposes, *The Dove*. But that was Jay for you, a large, gentle man with a surprising and, I thought, quite adjustable sense of humor.

We did not have long to wait. The sun was still about an hour above the horizon when Kenneth suddenly materialized beside me. Above us that vicious kite was showing its style as he worked it closer and closer to me. I glanced over at him. He looked bored.

Then out of the corner of my eye I saw Jay coming out from under the pier and throwing *The Dove* up into the strong breeze.

Holding the specially designed reel he'd rigged for me he came running across the sand. He said, "Drop that line." I let go of the string to the little paper kite I'd been flying. Jay shoved the big reel into my hands and said, "Now, fight him!"

The man with the devil kite looked startled. "What the hell is this?"

I said, "That's what I said to you the first time you cut me up. Now, fight, damn you!"

He had altitude on me. He looked over at me and said, "You're going to get cut up again. And quick."

Jay yelled into my ear: "Let out line! Quick!"

I barely avoided his first, narrowing swoop. Then I was above him and he moved away down the beach to give himself fighting room, letting out line as fast as I did. He said, "I'll cut your string for you and then you can see if that kite of yours can swim."

I knew better than that. My kite was carrying a thousand feet of 200-pound-test nylon cord and he'd break a razor blade before he cut my line.

But a problem I hadn't reckoned on was that his kite was colored a sky blue, deliberately tinted to make it hard to get a depth perception on against the sky over the sea. Time and again I tried to get a fix on the kite using the altitude strategy Jay had devised, only to realize that I was too low or too high. That gave Kenneth the opportunity to come swooping at me, taking hard runs with that devil kite of his against our red-and-white kite, which stood out like a sign post against the sky. That hadn't been Jay's fault; I had insisted on the two colors of plastic, the upper body red, the bottom white.

Kenneth hit me two hard licks, the last of which I could see had given me a slight tear in the right wing. But the heavy mylar plastic resisted increasing the tear under the force of the wind.

By now Kenneth had recognized Jay, who was staying by my side as we moved up and down the beach. He said, "You think he can beat me? Not with any kite you ever built."

Jay didn't say a word back to him. He just watched the sky, giving me quiet instructions. "Let out line. Now pull in. Now dive right. Now back up. Look out for him, here he comes. Dive left! Flutter!"

We had fought now for, I reckoned, some 45 minutes. The sky was beginning to change, becoming much bluer. In my ear Jay suddenly whispered, "Now, let him hit you."

I was startled. I said, without looking around, because you can't do that when you're fighting kites, "What!"

"Let him hit you! Do it! The kite will stand it!"

It hurt me, but I gave the devil kite an almost stationary target while he swooped in and gave *The Dove* a hard, direct blow. The kite shuddered through the string in my fingers, but was as steady as ever.

Close in my ear Jay said urgently, "Now give it line. Let it flutter like you're really hurt! Now! Now!"

I did as I was told, though I wasn't sure I understood. Kenneth dove his kite toward mine for the killing hit and Jay yelled, "Now pull in! Make it climb! Climb!"

Then I understood his strategy. The sky had turned dark enough so that I could see that light blue kite of his clearly outlined. I cranked on that big reel and *The Dove* rose upward as if it were going to heaven. The devil kite was right below me. Jay said, "Now dive and hit him!"

I brought *The Dove* down and hit him so hard with that ramming rod Jay had installed that I could hear the fabric of his kite rip. For a second the two kites were locked together, but then Kenneth jerked in line and pulled loose. The kites came away clear, both still flying.

But he'd lost that marvelous maneuverability he'd so wantonly flaunted. His kite was hurt and he knew it. He began running down the beach, reeling in line. There was a sea wall just down the beach and, if he got over it, I knew I'd lose him. I yelled at Jay, "Stop him!"

Jay went around both of us and got between Kenneth and his escape. He just stood there, his arms folded, and said: "Now the shoe's on the other foot. See how you like it."

He looked over at me desperately. For a moment there was sympathy in my heart, but then I realized I had to do the charitable thing. His kite was just hanging in the air. I maneuvered *The Dove* below him, lifted her up, and drove that ramming rod right straight through his horizontal strut.

We both stood there watching his line go limp as his kite slowly fell into the water. He turned to me and said, "You broke my kite."

"Hell, I feel bad about that," I said, "but I'm going to make it up to you."

I yelled for Jay and he came over and began reeling in *The Dove* while I walked back up the beach. I found the ball of twine connected to the Hi-Flier I'd dropped and took it back to Kenneth. I said, "Here. Here's another kite. Might be all wet when you drag it in, but then so are you."

He just stood there staring at me and said, again, "You broke my kite!"

I patted him on the shoulder. "Don't worry. For about three hundred bucks Jay will build you another. And if you're real nice about it he might throw in some fighting instructions."

Then Jay and I just walked away, carrying *The Dove*, kind of grinning.

We are thinking of offering her to the Air & Space Museum of the Smithsonian Institute.

20

Return to Piedras Negras

This was a visit back in time for me to see some old acquaintances of the matador bent whom I first met while writing an earlier story. Or at least that's what I went down there to write about. What resulted was completely unexpected and certainly unwelcome.

A lot of people don't know that being a sportswriter can be dangerous. Sometimes it can be almost as health-threatening as the injuries sustained by the athletes one covers. For instance, you can walk into a baseball locker room and nearly get punched out by a player who didn't like something you'd written about him. Or you could be at the press table which is courtside at a basketball game and suddenly catch a very large basketball player in your lap. Or be standing on the sidelines at a football game and find yourself the center of a swirling vortex of hard bodies and shoulder pads. You can even be innocently inspecting the landing area in the discus throw, have an official suddenly yell, "Look out!", and feel something dangerous go whizzing by your ear.

But all that ain't shucks to covering a bullfight. Or a *corrida de toros*, as it's more correctly known.

I'd always wanted to get up close to a *corrida de toros*. For some time, probably because I'd read too much Hemingway, I'd considered myself an aficionado. But I'd only seen it from afar and admittedly didn't know a great deal about it except what I'd read.

So, some years back, I took myself down to Piedras Negras, which is a Mexican border town across from Eagle Pass, Texas. Part of the attraction for me was the diverse talents of the two matadors. I wanted to see if I could tell the difference between them. One was Armillita, a journeyman torero who'd seen his best days. The other was Manolo Martinez, one of the few Special Class matadors of the three classes of bullfighters. But mainly I just wanted to get right up next to the action and see what it felt like.

Consequently, when I got to Piedras Negras I went to see the *impresario*, Rolando Ariste, and told him I wanted to be in the *callejón*, which is the narrow alleyway between the *barrera*, the wooden barricade that encircles the bullring, and the stands. I told him I didn't want to be in the stands and I didn't want to be in the press section. I wanted to be right down next to where it was happening.

Well, he gave me a sort of startled look and said that these bulls were Golderinas. Of course I knew enough to know that Spanish fighting bulls are called after the ranch they are from, not by breed as we do here in the States. I said I didn't give a damn where they were from, I still wanted to be right up next to the matadors down in the *callejón*.

Now, Señor Ariste spoke a little English and I spoke a little Spanish, but there were important gaps in between. It was this failure to communicate that turned out to be damn near fatal to me.

He kept trying to get across a point I was not getting. He said, looking worried, "*Toros son mariposos.*"

I just shook my head. Hell, I didn't care what color they were.

"Golondrina?" he said hopefully.

Again I shook my head. I now know what Senor Ariste was trying to tell me, but I was too intent at that time to investigate further.

He worried his head for a moment, trying to come up with a word in English that would tell me what I was letting myself in for, and finally just gave up. Whatever I wanted to do would be fine with him.

The situation did not start off too well the afternoon before the bullfight. It is the custom, the day before, for the matadors and their handlers and *cuadrillas* to go down and look the bulls over. I was staying in the same hotel with Armillita and Manolo and had already met them and they were willing for me to tag along.

The bulls were in a little corral just behind the *Plaza de Toros*. They looked pretty docile, just standing around, occasionally pawing the dirt. Of course I didn't know that they had steers turned in with them to keep them gentled.

I was not unfamiliar with bulls. I'd had a less than distinguished career as a rodeo cowboy, but there was something about these Spanish fighting bulls that was fascinating. They bore about the same similarity to a rodeo bull as a blunt instrument does to a stiletto. I determined I had to touch one.

The corral fence was about six feet high and made of wooden planks with spaces between the boards. One bull was standing near the fence, so I started climbing up, stretching out my hand. The bull backed away a foot. I climbed a step higher and then another, still stretching out my hand to touch the bull.

Next thing I knew I'd gone one step too high and lost my balance and went over the top and into the corral.

Well, I got out of there pretty fast, but it didn't matter. Not one of the bulls made a step toward me. The only damage was to my dignity which had already been pretty badly disfigured over the years. Going back to the hotel, Manolo told me that I would have been in serious danger if there had not been steers in with the bulls to keep them quiet. He said the bulls had a herdlike instinct and that the steers made them feel secure. He said a fighting bull was only truly dangerous when he was alone. I listened to what he had to say, but I was secretly thinking, "These babies ain't so tough."

I've thought things like that before and lived to regret them. Fortunately.

The bullring at Piedras Negras is about sixty yards across. The *barrera* is made of heavy wooden planks, each six inches thick and a bit over five feet tall. It is painted red except for the top, which is yellow. It is usually freshly painted just before each *corrida de toros*. I suppose that is to give it a festive air. The *callejón* is barely four feet wide. On the stand's side, a concrete wall rises some eight feet straight up with no hand holds or exits. In the *barrera*, spotted at strategic points around the ring there are openings of some four feet in width which are fronted by short, wooden barricades called *bulladeros*. These are intended to let the matadors and *banderillos* slip in and out to work the bull and to escape if necessary. However, the space between the *bulladero* and the *barrera* is only wide enough to let someone built like a matador or a ballerina slip through.

I tell you these things now, just in case you've never seen a bullring, so as not to stall your enjoyment of the fun I was about to have with such tiresome details during a situation that was happening just a little faster than even I could see it.

And I was on the spot. Right there, so to speak.

Manolo, as was his right as senior matador, took the first bull. I leaned over the *barrera* watching. He did, I suppose, a very credible job. I didn't have anything to compare him with so I was anxious for Armillita to enter the ring.

I believe Manolo got an ear. Or a tail. Or some such. Maybe the whole carcass for all I knew.

Then Armillita's bull came skidding into the ring. He was a sleek, fast-moving fighting machine with wide-open horns, the kind that bull fighters prefer since they are less likely to inflict a *cornada*, a goring, than closed-horned bulls.

Of course I didn't know any of this then so I just hung over the *barrera*, contentedly watching Armillita put the bull through his paces. Finally he took him down to the far end of the bullring, to my right, to lead him to the *picadores*. At this point my attention sort of wandered and I looked off to my left for a second. When I looked back I saw a sight I couldn't quite figure out. I saw a photographer, with about sixty pounds of cameras around his neck, suddenly go halfway over the *barrera*, balancing on his midriff. Then I saw another couple of figures pop up and get astride the barrier. I was wondering what the hell had possessed these people. I glanced into the bullring and saw Armillita running my way. Somewhat idly I wondered what he'd done with the bull, which was nowhere in sight. Then I heard a sort of swelling noise from the crowd and I wondered what they were so hot about. Then I took a look down the *callejón*.

And there, rounding the curve of the alley, on my side of the *barrera*, was the stuff nightmares are made of. About twelve feet away from me, coming at his top speed, was the most red-eyed, slobber-mouthed, sharp-pointed-horned, with-intent-to-kill bull I had ever seen.

In that instant I realized several things. The first, of course, was that I was in a hell of a mess with nowhere to go. But I also realized what Senor Ariste had been trying to tell me. *Mariposa* means butterfly. *Golondrina* means swallow. He was attempting to tell me that these Goldorina bulls are famous for taking to the air and jumping the *barrera*. If he could have just had enough English to say, "Good God, man, you don't want to be down there. You'll have a fighting bull in your hair in no time."

By now that bull had seen me and he was in no mood to be reasonable. I think he was already a little irritated with the proceedings and looking for someone to take it out on. I saw him lower that head and take dead aim at the only body I own.

I read somewhere that the standing high jump was discontinued as an Olympic event in 1912 and that Ray Ewry retired with the record at 5'5". I think his record is safe—if I'd topped it I probably would have knocked the crossbar off. I say that because I landed on the other side of the *barrera* with fresh yellow paint on the leg of the jeans that I was wearing. But I made that jump in cowboy boots with a cup of Coke in my hand. I don't know what style I used; certainly it wasn't the Foxbury Flop. I'd been a sprinter and a hurdler, not a high jumper, but it is amazing what a bull can teach you in a very short time.

I ended up sitting on the sand with my back against the *barrera*, panting and sending up prayers. Behind me I could hear the crowd and it certainly sounded to me like they were having a slight laugh at my expense. I stood up and began to look for a way to get out of the bullring with what little was left of my dignity.

At that instant the blasted bull took it into his head to jump *back* into the ring. Now he had any number of targets to choose from; there was Armillita; there was the *picador* on his horse; there were two *banderillas*. Instead he circled that ring and once again focused on me. The *bulladero* was just to my left. I knew I couldn't jump the barrier again so I began trying to squeeze through the tiny opening. But it wasn't made for men who weigh 200 pounds. And the bull was coming. Armillita was coming too, but the bull was coming faster. I heard him yell "*¡Capote!*" and one of his *banderillas* threw me a cape. I grabbed it, wadded the big thing up, and threw it right at the charging bull's head. Magically it opened up and covered his face like I'd dropped a curtain. He stopped, confused. In that instant I sucked in everything I had and squeezed behind that *bulladero*.

I don't know how Armillita got that cape off the bull's horns and went on with his business, but I can tell you that a Mexican crowd, some of whom have spent a day's pay to go to the *fiesta de toros*, are not interested in seeing some gringo get in the way. Consequently

I was greeted with a small shower of seat cushions. I have been told this was an accolade, but I don't believe it.

That night in the hotel I went by Manolo's room. His door was open and he was seated, surrounded by admirers. He saw me and waved, but I just ducked my head and went on to my room. I needed to talk to him, but I wasn't really in the mood at that moment.

Somewhat later I was lying on the bed, staring at the ceiling and trying to assess the joys of abject fear and total embarrassment, when the door suddenly burst open and a set of bull horns, backed by a man, followed by several more, came crowding in. I had been so unnerved that afternoon that I admit to jumping off the bed when I saw the horns. But it was Manolo and a few of his friends. They'd taken the horns off the wall of the restaurant downstairs. He came into the room grinning and clicking a pair of scissors. I knew what it meant. A matador wears a pigtail, a very short pigtail that he pins up under his *montera*, the black, leaded hat he wears into the ring. It's his badge of honor. Traditionally, when a matador retires he cuts his pigtail. It is a sign that he is no longer going into the ring.

Manolo had come to cut my pigtail. I think he was trying to tell me to stay out of the bullring from then on. I could not have agreed with him more.

The only problem was that I didn't have a pigtail. I'm a shorthair and always have been. We couldn't find anything to cut. Well, we had some iced tea and cookies and studied the problem and finally came up with a solution. Took a lot of iced tea but we figured it out.

Manolo cut off my cowlick.

Which, in view of my proceedings with the bulls that afternoon, seemed very fitting.

21

An Affair for Gentlemen

As you read this you'll probably realize that this was the most uncomfortable twenty-four hours I ever spent outside of a hospital.

What you don't know is that, because of the good response we got to the story, Bill Broyles proposed I write about a six-day sailing race from Corpus Christi to some port in Mexico.

At that point I figured I had lost my touch and wasn't getting my point across as a writer.

Of course you must understand that it was the same Bill Broyles who once proposed I spend thirty days in the Harris County jail to do an investigative report.

If he'd lived in the fifteenth century, he could have found work with the Spanish Inquisition.

I was assigned to the crew of the *Barbarian,* a yacht as appropriately named for the sport of ocean racing as any in the fleet. The race would begin in Galveston, take a southerly reach to a point off Freeport, turn east 35 miles out in the Gulf of Mexico, and then complete the triangle with a leg back into Galveston harbor. It would, depending on the winds, take anywhere from twenty to thirty hours and cover a straight-line distance of 107 miles. But, of course, yacht races are not sailed in straight lines.

The *Barbarian* is a forty-one-foot, two-ton, sloop-rigged, custom-built racing yacht owned and skippered by Houston orthopedic surgeon Don Lazarz. There were eight of us in the crew. There was a professional yachtsman from Australia named Bruce, who'd spent the last year transporting boats about the world and racing for anyone who could afford him. There was Harris, an MIT graduate and a naval architect for Exxon; John, a mechanical engineer for the same company; Herb, an advertising executive; Riley, who has something to do with tax forms, but mainly races; and Donny, the skipper's son. All were young, tan, and athletic. The last member of the crew will go nameless because he does not figure in this narrative. He was a friend of the skipper who'd come along to see if he wanted to take up yachting, but, two hours out, he was violently seasick and spent the balance of the race hanging over the aft railing. In the end they buckled him into a safety harness and secured him to a stanchion so he wouldn't slide overboard as the deck tilted violently back and forth. Other than that he was ignored. During the race Riley's back went out and he too was ignored, no one even bothering to help him below.

Which is partly by way of saying that yacht racing, especially ocean racing, is a very complicated, very strenuous, very challenging sport carried on in nigh intolerable conditions. It is not at all a sedentary activity where people sit around drinking beer while the wind fills the sails and the bow cleaves smoothly through the waves. Instead it is a world of pitching decks, instant decisions, innumerable sail changes, cuts and bruises, ruthless tactics, and waves that crash rather than cleave.

It is also very big in Texas. I was told by any number of people that there are more sailing vessels along the Texas coast than anywhere else on the Gulf of Mexico, including Florida. I have reason to believe this. About a year ago I had gone down to the Caribbean to do a story for *Sports Illustrated* on yacht hijacking by dope runners. Calling at various yacht clubs, I tried to find local sailors who could perhaps give me a lead. But everyone I approached was from Galveston or Corpus Christi or some other Texas port.

There are all sorts of sailing in Texas, all the way from the board boats to big ocean-going cruisers and ocean racers like the *Barbarian*. They range in price from about $400 all the way up to whatever you want to pay. We are only concerned here with offshore racing, ocean racing, which is handled by the Texas Ocean Racing Circuit and is sanctioned by the U.S. Yacht Racing Union. Also I'll be using a number of nautical terms that I won't bother to explain. But it is important that you learn the weather side and leeward side of the boat. The weather (or windward) side is the side from which the wind is blowing. Leeward is the opposite—the side that tilts or heels in response to the wind. The more level a boat is, the better it sails, so any crew member who is not occupied should be as high up on the weather side as he can be, preferably hanging over the side. Racing is not comfortable. As a matter of fact it is damn uncomfortable. The deck of a racing sloop, even one as big as the *Barbarian*, is covered with spindles and knobs and cleats and a great many other hard things. And when the boat tacks, coming about, the deck reverses tilt in a great hurry and going to weather can sometimes be like scrambling up a rising rocky wall. If you need to move around, you spot something you think you can grab, then you lunge for it and try to hold on.

But then racing isn't meant to be comfortable, any more than football or boxing is meant to be comfortable. After we'd been out about six hours Herb was in the cabin, exhausted, lying in one of the leeward bunks because the weather bunks are nearly impossible to stay in even with the sideboards. The skipper came down to check his chart and saw him. "Get to a weather bunk, Herb," he said.

Herb said, "Aw, Skipper, I'm all right. I'm give out."

Lazarz said firmly, "That hasn't got anything to do with it. That's not what it's all about. Now get to weather!"

Herb did, because if you're going to race, you race—and lying in a leeward bunk isn't racing. Even that much weight in the wrong place can cost a tenth of a knot and that can sometimes mean the difference between winning and losing.

The *Barbarian* cost over $200,000, but she has very few bunks and a tiny galley. Even the door from the head has been removed to save weight. But that doesn't matter. You don't have time to eat or sleep, and if you could sit on the can under sailing conditions, you could make your living riding bucking horses. She carries sixteen sails and each one, bagged, is about the size of a coffin and, wet, weighs about as much. Most of the inside space of the vessel is taken up with these sails, and a good bit of time is spent dragging them up on deck and then taking them back down. I had one dropped on me through the forward hatch and it knocked me flat.

There were forty-one boats in the race in five classes. The *Barbarian* rated at two tons, though that has nothing to do with her actual weight, as she weighs four times that much. There were three other boats in our class. Then there were the one-tonners, half-tonners, and two cruising classes. In the race each boat would be trying to win its class, but mainly it would be trying to win fleet. The race is run on a handicap system. The *Barbarian* was the highest-rated boat; consequently we were giving up time to the rest of the fleet. We weren't afraid of any of the boats in our class, in fact expected to beat them easily, but for the fleet win we were apprehensive about the one-tonners. *Ambush* and *Quick*, each of which we were giving 44 minutes. We were even more concerned about the half-tonners, particularly *Rolling Time*, which we spotted 2 hours and 23 minutes. She was a dark horse, a lake sailer that had been trailered down from Fort Worth. No one knew much about her, but those who'd seen her in practice said she looked extremely fast in light air and even appeared to be able to go to weather some. Two hours and 23 minutes was a lot of time.

We formed that morning in the Galveston yacht basin, the boats coming out of their slips and milling around the committee boat and the starting line. The air was very light, a subject of concern, especially to us. We wanted wind, and lots of it, preferably three weather legs, for that's where a big boat like *Barbarian* is at her best.

But the wind held light, and after an hour there was some doubt whether there could be a race at all. Starting time came and there was a postponement. Boats tacked back and forth, drifting aimlessly under a sun that had, by now, become quite hot. On our boat we discussed what sails we'd use for the first leg out of the channel. This was mostly between Bruce and the skipper since all the decisions would be made by them. Assignments were reiterated and alternatives proposed for every conceivable eventuality. Everyone was nervous and tense.

Mainly, though, we were worried. The wind did not blow, and we listened anxiously to the marine radio hoping for some good news of a front passing or a storm or anything that might give us a hard blow. We were the class of the fleet and expected to win, but we couldn't do it in light air.

Finally there was a freshet and then a light breeze that began to increase, and our spirits rose. The warning cannon sounded on the committee boat and then, ten minutes later, sounded again, and the first class was off. The small boats go first, then the cruising classes, one-tonners, and then us. We went in ten-minute intervals, all of which was figured into the time handicap.

We got off to a bad start. We had hoped to tack back and forth and come up to the starting line seconds after the cannon went off to start us. But just as we approached the line, *Compadre,* one of the boats in our class, hove in on our port bow, forcing us wide of the committee boat, and we had to shear off and come about. Consequently we were the last boat in the fleet off the mark.

Out ahead of us the other boats were beating their way out of the channel, their sails startlingly white against the midday sky. The air was holding light and we began to tack back and forth as we sought to get the boat driving. We were running under mainsail (which would not change during the voyage) and a light #1 headsail (which would be changed many, many times).

I had seen these same people around yacht clubs all over the coast and they had seemed like such *nice* people. To my pleasant surprise there had been none of that money snobbishness you sometimes find around country clubs. I remember thinking that was because the sea is so unforgiving of any carelessness or neglect, it creates a certain democratic bond, a feeling of all being in the same boat, as it were. I had had drinks the evening before with Lazarz and Bruce in the Lakewood Yacht Club and they were so pleasant, so well-spoken and friendly.

But now we were racing, and, as we came up on our first tack: "Goddammit, move, move, move!"

"Get on that winch, Herb! Grind, you sonofabitch! Grind!"

"Get the halyard! There's the halyard, you dumbhead! Christ!"

"Goddammit, get that sheet home!"

I was tailing on the starboard winch and I let go the halyard and we nearly lost a sail. Lazarz was at the helm and he screamed: "Get that sonofabitch out of there!"

It was all rushed, frantic, wild.

Bruce yelled from the foredeck: "Get up the bloody stays'l! Herb, John! Move your bloody asses!"

Lazarz yelled from the helm: "Let's don't slot that yet, Bruce."

"We've bloody got to, mate!"

"Let's get out of the channel first."

"Not right."

So we slotted the staysail. During the race there would be many conflicts between Bruce and the skipper about sail changes and such. In almost every case, Bruce prevailed. In fairness to Lazarz,

I'm sure he was under no illusions about who was the better sailor. Racing was Bruce's business and we all knew it. But when you've invested $200,000 in a boat and are nominally the skipper, you'd at least like to have your say.

We were beginning to pass other boats. Even in the light air the *Barbarian* was driving well under the headsail and staysail. We passed *Compadre* and everyone turned to give them a sour look.

Harris asked: "Are you going to protest?"

And Don growled back: "Protest what? He had the right-of-way."

Bruce said: "Not if you'd kept her headed up."

"And what? Rammed the committee boat?"

We reached the end of the channel and came about, turning now for the long southerly reach to Freeport. Away from the land, the breeze began to freshen, and the wind gauge on the instrument panel over the cabin door rose to fifteen knots and held steady. Already we had passed all the boats in our class and were beginning to catch the one-tonners. Ahead of us, boats well out to sea began to set their spinnakers. A spinnaker is the huge, multi-colored balloon-like sail billowing out in front of yachts. You use it only if the wind is favoring you and you don't have to tack. Small in the distance we could see the bright sails suddenly come blossoming out from the leading yachts.

"All right, mates," Bruce sang out, "let's do it! Let's get the bloody heads'l down! Throw that line, Donny! John, get that chute up here. Move it, lads, move it!"

Again, all that rushed, frantic madness. Clinging to the weather edge of the deck and watching the swirl of ropes and lines and halyards, I couldn't see how they could possibly bring any order out of such confusion. But in moments the staysail lay crumpled on the foredeck and Herb, at the mast, was frantically cranking up the spinnaker while Harris and John were setting it from midships. It popped out, blooming, a tribute to our boat since none of the other two-tonners could carry a spinnaker as quickly as we could, and we felt a sudden surge as the huge sail pulled the boat forward. We watched the knot meter above the companionway door. It resembles a digital clock, only the numbers are bigger. Our speed climbed from 5.52 to 5.73 to 6.00 (a little cheer went up as we passed 6) and then on up to 6.55. I hate to think what that gadget cost, but it is marvelous. It gives you instant changes in speed in hundredths of knots, and you can make your sail corrections accordingly.

Soon, however, the wind began to shift, and we started having trouble with the spinnaker. It was losing some of its tautness, and sometimes, as the lee rail dipped under a wave, the lower edge of the sail would drag the water. Don said quietly, "All right, let's get the reacher out. Get ready to get it up."

Bruce said, "Not yet."

"At least get the sonofabitch on deck."

"We ought to keep the chute up a bit longer, mate."

"Goddammit, I can't hold it!" The boat was heeling dangerously, the lee rail now almost continuously under water.

So the change was made, fighting down the spinnaker, almost losing it as one end came loose, and then battling to raise the reacher, a huge, light headsail. This time Lazarz had been right, for as soon as the reacher was up, the knot meter began to creep past the 7 mark. Bruce, glancing at the knot meter, said, "By Christ, Skipper, when you're right, you're bloody right."

It was during this exchange that Riley's back went out. One moment he was standing in the midships cockpit and the next he was bent over screaming with pain. He half-fell, half-stumbled down the companionway steps into the cabin. Someone told Lazarz that Riley's back had gone out.

"Yeah," the orthopedic surgeon said, "it does that."

By now there were only a few boats ahead of us: *Ambush, Quick, Rolling Time,* and another half-tonner far out to sea. I noticed Lazarz letting the boat fall off course, bearing down on *Quick.* I asked him what he had in mind.

"I'm going to smother the bastard," he said.

By that he meant he was going to place our boat in between *Quick* and the breeze, taking the wind out of their sails while we kept ours driving. They saw us coming and their skipper desperately tried to change course. But we were too fast for them. Little by little we crept up until we were broadside, only about thirty yards away. We could see their sails start to collapse.

"Let 'em eat a little of our garbage," Lazarz said, and laughed. He made minute changes, keeping our boat driving, but hovering over them as long as he could. Over on *Quick* they were not exactly shaking their fists at us, but, while they made frantic sail adjustments, they would shoot hard looks our way. Then we pulled on ahead, carefully holding off their windward bow so that all they got was the turbulent backwash off our own sails. We left them slowed in the water, their sails fluttering.

"Beautiful, Skip!" Bruce said. "Bloody beautiful!"

Then we did the same thing to *Ambush*. They took it more stoically, beginning to harden sail while we were still making up on them. Not one of their crew even glanced our way. We left them in the same circumstances as we had *Quick*.

I wondered if that was quite fair.

"It's racing," was all Lazarz said.

Rolling Time was standing out a half mile seaward of us. There was a brief discussion about whether we should go for her, but it was decided it wouldn't be worth the course change.

"The hell with her," Lazarz said. "If we get a good weather leg on the second course we'll lose her anyway."

It was coming twilight, and behind us the rest of the fleet was spread out. Some of the boats were still close enough that we could see their hulls, but mostly all we saw were the white sails leaning to leeward. Even though to win we still had a lot of time to make up, it was exhilarating to be out in front with nothing ahead but a clear expanse of water.

Bruce relieved Don at the wheel. He got up stiff and cramped. "We've got to hold 230 degrees to make the marker," he said, "but I'll get another fix in a moment."

They had the spinnaker bagged now, and I dragged it downstairs into the cabin. Riley was lying in one of the cramped weather bunks where sails are stowed for ballast. There wasn't room to shove the sail in because of Riley, so I was about to put it in on the leeward side when Don came down.

"Here," he said, "put that up on the weather side. We'll be on this reach another three or four hours and weather side isn't going to change before we need that sail again."

"But there's no room in there," I said. "Riley's in there."

"Then put it on top of him."

I thought he was kidding and said so.

"Hell no," he said. "Here, give me that." Lazarz is a big ,powerful man and he grabbed the sail and threw it in on top of the unfortunate Riley.

"Good God, Don," I said, "he's hurt!"

"He can push it out of the way." Then he turned away and went to the navigation table.

I looked in under the bulkhead. Riley had managed to push the sail over far enough to get it out of his face. He gave me a weak grin.

It was night now, and the sea was roughening. Looking back we could see the distance we were putting on the other boats. Toward land an interesting situation was developing. A big cruising class boat, the *Nimbus*, was sailing well in, three or four miles toward the shore, but she was running almost on a head with us. I asked and Bruce just shrugged. "She's too low. By the time she points up enough to make the marker she'll be three, four miles behind us."

But she wasn't. I watched her as it got darker and darker and the moon came out, keeping her in sight by her running lights. She kept pointing up into the wind while, at the same time, running abreast of us. An hour after dark she was only a mile downwind, still holding her own. Don came out of the cabin where he'd been taking a fix and studied her. We were approaching San Luis Pass. "He's taking a chance. It gets awfully shallow in there."

We were on a long reach, legging it on a course for the Freeport marker, and the boat had become comparatively quiet. We were all huddled up on the weather aft corner of the boat, keeping our weight as far back as possible—except for Harris, the sail trimmer, who was up on the foredeck shining a flashlight up at the telltales. These are little strings attached to the leading edges of the sails. Ideally they are supposed to stream out without fluttering next to the sail. Occasionally he would call back, "Take in an inch on the stays'l" or "Let out a turn on the header."

Then we would all watch the knot meter anxiously, hoping to pick up another hundredth of a knot, feeling good if we succeeded, or yelling out if the speed fell off. It was incredible how minute and continual the sail adjustments were. In the dark behind us, we could see the faint glow of the flashlights as other foredeckmen on the trailing boats checked their sails. Occasionally the skipper would peer back through his binoculars, trying to determine how our lead was progressing.

It had become cold by now and, one by one, the crew went down to put on heavier clothes. Once, Herb and John lingered too long in the cabin, and Lazarz yelled down: "Okay, you guys, if you haven't got business down there get your asses back up here. You're not doing the boat a damn bit of good down there."

And, when they didn't respond quickly enough, he yelled: "Goddammit! Get up here."

There would be those moments of yelling, shoving, cursing, frantic madness, when everyone was at each other's throats. And then would come the moments of quiet, with only the slosh and slap of the sea and the creak of the running gear, and they would talk quietly among themselves, making small nautical jokes. Most of them had raced with Don many times before. In fact, Harris had missed only three races on the boat. I asked him why he did it. He's a quiet, athletic, bearded type and he looked at me in astonishment. "Because I love it," he said. "Otherwise I wouldn't do it."

"Why? You can't call this fun."

"I suppose every man has his own definition of fun."

He had me there, for even as cold and cramped and bruised as I was, I found myself beginning to enjoy it.

Four miles from the marker at Freeport there was another heated crisis. The wind had fallen off to ten knots and was blowing at a 60-degree angle in relation to the boat. Harris and Bruce wanted to set a star rigging, which meant raising a smaller-cut spinnaker. Lazarz vacillated.

"It's bloody perfect for a star," Bruce said, standing on the foredeck with his hands on his hips. "Let's get the sails up."

"But goddammit, it's only four miles, less than that now, to the buoy."

Then there was a mixed discussion about the heavy #1 headsail and the light #1 and whether the port halyards would be free or the starboard or which tack we'd be on. It went too fast for me to follow. The main argument seemed to center around whether they'd want the heavy #1 up on the second leg, which all hoped would be a weather leg. But the breeze was holding light and Lazarz was fearful we wouldn't be able to run under the heavy #1 on the weather leg. In the end they compromised by putting up the heavy #1 before we rounded the mark. Bruce said, "What the bloody hell, if we're wrong, we can get the light back up in a flash."

Surprisingly, *Nimbus* had made it to windward and, in the dark, had pulled ahead of us. She turned the marker, a flashing beacon, just as we arrived at it, but no one seemed to be concerned. "She can't go to weather," Harris said contemptuously.

Now we were on the long leg out into the Gulf, bound for a drilling platform thirty-five miles away. The wind was freshening and seemed to be swinging to the north. Jubilation swept us. We wanted weather, tacking weather. A weather leg would lengthen the race; it would mean a lot of tacks and we could sail five points closer to the wind than any other boat in the fleet and sail it faster. Consequently, with just one good weather leg we could make up all the time we were giving the other boats. That ability was one of the reasons the boat had cost $200,000. But it's no good if the wind won't cooperate.

It had grown late and most of the crew had gone below. Harris had been given the wheel and only he and John, who was trimming sail, and I were on deck. Of course our useless ninth crew member was still slumped aft over the transom. Occasionally Don would come up and fretfully check the course and the wind direction and our speed. We were on a fetch, a long reach that would carry us to our second marker. Lazarz was worried. We weren't getting the weather leg. Only once did he lose his frown. He looked back at his friend who was throwing up over the rail for the numberless time and made a bad joke. But his laugh was dry and he soon turned his attention back to the situation of the boat.

We never did get our beat, making it to the platform instead on one long reach. Occasionally Harris, who loves to steer, would watch the knot meter creep above 7 and yell, "God, we're streaking! We're screaming!"

But we all knew that the light boats behind us were screaming also.

Sometime early in the morning we turned the drilling platform, a well-lighted skyscraper incongruously adrift in all that black water. We could hear the hum of the huge diesels and the throb of heavy engines. A few roughnecks leaned over the railing and watched us curiously, perhaps wondering what the hell we thought we were doing.

We were on the homebound leg and the crew was weighed down with worry. The air was very light. When I had been assigned to the boat, David Whitaker, the race chairman, had predicted confidently that the *Barbarian* would win. She had just come in from racing in southern waters, against class boats from all over the world, and had done very well. But now it didn't look so good. With the coming of dawn, we could see sails behind us. They were far back, but we should have had the water to ourselves. We ran under a spinnaker for a while, but the air was too light, and we finally went back to a reacher and entered the channel under that.

An hour later we went into the harbor and swept past the end of the dock where the committee was now set up. They fired the cannon to signify we were the first boat to finish, then we backed into a slip and tied up.

For a while everyone just sat there feeling the gentle rocking of the boat. It felt strange to be at rest after all that pounding motion. Finally Don heaved himself up. "Well, let's go down and get the bad news."

We walked down and stood around with the committee. "Nice race," Whitaker said. "Lovely race. God, you were tearing along on that first leg."

"Yeah," Don said sourly.

The answer wasn't long in coming. *Ambush* came tacking in, beating us on corrected time by 3 minutes and 25 seconds. We were now second in the fleet, even though we'd won our class.

Then *Quick* came in, dropping us to third. They added insult to injury. After crossing the finish line, they came about, and as they sailed by the committee, one of the crewmen yelled over and asked, "Did we beat *Barbarian?*" Apparently they hadn't forgotten our little maneuver the evening before. Third didn't last long. *Rolling Time* unexpectedly appeared, sweeping across the line, chewing up, with their handicap, the entire field.

"A goddam lake boat," Don said disgustedly.

Bruce said, "Christ, they must have sailed like witches."

We retreated to the *Barbarian*. Over the years I have been in the locker rooms of many losing teams—football, baseball, basketball. The atmosphere was the same in the cabin of the *Barbarian*. In the locker rooms you'd hear one phrase, perhaps, "God, if we just hadn't fumbled" or "God, if we just hadn't thrown the ball away." Here it was, "God, if we'd just had one weather leg! Just one goddam beat!" That was said over and over.

So we sat around drinking beer for a while. Occasionally someone would try a joke. Harris said, looking at Herb, "Well, at least we didn't have to use our human fender." I wondered what that was, and Don said, "Last year a boat was bearing down on us, and I yelled for someone to fend it off. Herb missed with the boat hook and fell down in between and got his pelvis crushed."

"Got his. . . . Did what?"

"Got his pelvis crushed."

For lack of something better to say I asked, "Well, Doc, did you treat him for it? Since it was your boat?"

"Yes," he said. He thought a moment. " And I think I collected on his insurance."

We were all very tired. After a time Don said, "Well, let's go home."

I said, "I'm sorry you lost, Skipper."

He shrugged. "That's racing."

But I wanted to know more. "What *is* racing?"

He thought for a moment. Then he shrugged again. "Sometimes it's like standing under an ice cold shower slowly tearing up hundred dollar bills."

22

Pneumatic Cushioning and the All-American Boy

The first year after Pierce Holt left college he played in the Super Bowl. His team, the San Francisco 49ers, won. Pierce Holt, a man who had wondered if he was even going to be drafted, now has a Super Bowl ring. They tell me those things are worth about $30,000. That's pretty nice for a kid who was worried about repaying his student loans.

None of that has anything to do with the following.

I t was Pierce Holt's humility, and modesty, and disgusting All-American boyishness that caused me to get three cracked ribs.

And that's not right. Not as far as I'm concerned.

Well, maybe the fact that he is 6'5", weighs 285 pounds, and can bench press a Studebaker had a little something to do with it. And that he was drafted by the San Francisco 49ers and was the thirty-ninth draft pick overall and that he can run a 4.9 forty-yard dash. And got paid an enormous amount of money because he plays football so well and likes to hurt quarterbacks and running backs and anybody else that gets in his way.

Those may have been contributing factors, but it is my considered belief that my cracked ribs came as a direct result of his all-around too-good-to-be-true humility and niceness.

Real niceness. Real disgusting niceness.

Off the field, of course. Like the TV announcers say about those monsters who commit mayhem for sixty minutes and then apparently undergo some sort of metamorphosis and become Ward Cleaver in their real lives.

A standard cliche that, by the way, I'd never believed because I'd known too many of those sixty-minute monsters and I knew a good many of them were full-time monsters.

But Pierce was the first I'd ever gotten to study in the embryo stage, and the first time I sat down to hear his story I had to put my hand over my face several times to keep from laughing.

Nobody could be that swell and good and just gosh darn all-around fine.

Pierce played high school football at Lamar Consolidated, a 4A school near Houston. He wasn't even a starter and, when he graduated as a lanky 180-pound defensive end no college, not even a junior college, seemed to know he was alive.

But Pierce wanted to play college football. The fact that he was relatively small and relatively slow and relatively unathletic did not seem to have occurred to him. Consequently, he set out on the most direct path he could think of to realize his dream of first, college ball and then, the pros.

I don't think he was planning on the Pro Bowl at that point, but I'm not completely sure.

Anyway, naturally the first thing he did was get married. Anybody knows that will make you a better football player. After that he got a job and then enrolled at night school at a small junior college. Probably he didn't notice that night schools don't field teams.

But that's beside the point. What he *also* did was start going to the gym, working with weights. And he started running to improve his speed. In between doing that he was conducting one-man football practices with himself and reading all the books on the subject he could lay his hands on and watching all the film he could find.

And growing.

He started creeping up there, slowly but surely. First he got to 200 pounds, then 220, then 240 and pretty soon he was up there in the serious range.

He also got taller, finally topping out at the six-foot-five-inch mark after two years.

That should have been enough, but ol' Pierce believes in overkill, so he just kept working and sweating for another two years, being dead certain there wasn't an ounce of freeloading fat on his body. He figured that any weight he was carrying was there to do a job and no exceptions allowed.

Finally, four years out of high school, he picked up the phone and started calling coaches. He was then twenty-two years old and hadn't played a down of football for four years.

Now, I ask you, who would have the gall to start hunting for a football scholarship with those qualifications and expect a favorable reaction?

Well, Pierce, for one. He said he thought it was worth a try and he'd just up and give it one.

Naturally he went at it in his best no-sell, down-home, good-ol'-boy manner, saying "yessir" and "nosir" and not even bothering to lie a little about some experience he might have had that couldn't be checked.

Just told the truth. Even told a coach at Baylor who asked about his speed that his *wife* had clocked him in the forty-yard dash.

Obviously the man didn't so much hang up the phone on him as nearly choke to death laughing.

But ol' Pierce just kept running up his phone bill and learning how to take "no" real good.

Until he finally ran across another rather unusual man: Jerry Vandergriff, head coach at Angelo State in San Angelo, Texas. Now Angelo State is not the Southwest Conference and it's not the Big Ten, but they play some serious football at Angelo even though it's an NCAA II school. For a couple of quarters, until they get out-depthed, schools like Angelo can take on just about anybody in the country, but they've only got forty five scholarships and a limited budget, so coaches like Jerry Vandergriff are pretty tight with their money. But he was intrigued when Pierce called.

He told me, "Frankly, I didn't believe him at first. I've known a lot of dedicated football players, but I'd never heard of *anybody* laying out for four years and working out on their own just for a tryout. But I thought, what the hell, it's worth a plane ticket and a visit. And what if he *is* telling the truth? If I passed up something like that I'd be kicking myself from here to Dallas."

So Pierce came down and Vandergriff was impressed enough to not only give him a scholarship, but to also arrange other financing, because by now Pierce, knowing the surest route to the pros, had a wife, plus two children.

Pierce rewarded Vandergriff by making All-American his junior and senior years.

But that's not really what this story is about. This story is about my cracked ribs and how I got them.

Pierce started coming around his senior season. He'd heard that I was conversant with a number of coaches in the pros and some of the scouts for the combines and he wanted to find out what I thought.

Well, I thought plenty from what I'd seen on the field, but I just couldn't buy this humble, polite, gee-whiz exterior and transmit it to pro football. He wouldn't, for instance, even call my wife or me by our first names. It was always "Mr." and "Mrs."

But what got me the most was, did I think he'd be offered enough to pay off his student loans, which were worrying him no end?

His student loans?

Here was a guy who was probably going to sign for the equivalent of a plumber's lifetime earnings, talking to me about his student loans.

I'd already called a few friends in the pro circles and I knew Pierce was going high, but nothing I could say would reassure him.

Finally I just got fed up, and made a rash challenge.

Nothing new for me.

He'd been sitting on one of our small couches when I decided I'd had enough. I'd gone over and grabbed him by the collar and shaken him. Now, that is no mean feat with Pierce. Generally the one doing the shaking ends up getting shaken the most. But it was complicated by my wife's reaction. She'd been convinced from the first day Pierce walked through our front door that he was likely to bring the roof down on our heads just by his very size and here I was grabbing him, attempting to get his attention by jerking him around. She figured that was the end of the couch. His sitting there was enough to bring it to its end and she certainly didn't see any point in my aggavating the already dangerous situation.

Now, my wife is a Yankee who went to a school whose main sport was field hockey and she'd never seen anyone like Pierce. True, she'd seen a few pro football players in the house, but they were linebackers and, while she'd been awed, Pierce was something else.

So, between fighting her off and trying to get Pierce's attention, I had a more than difficult time getting my point across.

But I had finally said, "All right, Pierce, I've had enough of this. I don't think you're tough enough or mean enough to play pro football. Oh, sure, I've seen you bounce a few quarterbacks around and I've seen you gather up a cloud of people and sort them out until you found the one with the ball, but I'm talking *mean*! Pro football players are *mean*. And you can't come around here with that mouth full of namby-pamby and convince me you're mean."

He'd said, "Yes sir, Mr. Tippette."

I'd said, "That's exactly what I mean. You are still too damn respectful. All right, here's what we're going to do. You and I are going to suit up and I'm going to accept ten passes from any quarterback you can find. You try and dislodge the ball from me. Knock me loose from it! Then I'll know. If you'll hit a fifty-year-old man you are truly mean and you've got a chance in the pros."

My chest had been heaving as I'd finished, mostly from the effort of trying to shake Pierce, but I thought I'd meant it.

Of course I'd had several glasses of iced tea at that point and iced tea tends to make me overreach myself.

Pierce had said, "Oh, no, Mr. Tippette, I couldn't do that."

I'd said, grimly, "You damn well will do it!"

My wife had just looked at me and shaken her head. Didn't say anything. Didn't have to because, by the time Pierce left, the iced tea was starting to wear off, and plain old cold reality was setting in.

Well, we did it. Pierce called me one day and said it was all set and I said, "What's all set?"

So he told me. I thought maybe we'd both forgotten.

My wife didn't say anything, just gave me the gimlet eye.

Came the time and Pierce and I started suiting up over at Angelo State's athletic facilities. There were a lot of people in the dressing room, photographers (obviously drawn to the event in the same way they like to shoot train wrecks), friends, and some people who apparently bore me ill will from past misdeeds. I didn't particularly notice. All I could see was Pierce getting bigger and bigger and it had nothing to do with the pads he was putting on.

I didn't have much trouble with the pads; they were still pretty much the same even though the last time I'd had any on was for a charity game in El Dorado, Arkansas, back in 1960. But I did get slightly alarmed when Randy Matthews, the Angelo State trainer, came over to inflate the padding in my helmet.

I said, "What the hell is this?"

He said, "Pneumatic cushioning."

I said, "Pneumatic cushioning? What the hell happened to plain old foam rubber?"

I think he was trying to be diplomatic or kind or some such because he said, "Well, this is sort of a new innovation. Cuts down on head injuries the way the game is played today."

He also seemed a little sad that I wouldn't wear any rib pads. I'd said, "What? And cut down on my speed? No thanks."

He'd just looked at me and didn't say anything else.

Finally we were suited out and Pierce was standing up, stamping his feet on the concrete, apparently making certain his cleats would stand the strain he was about to put on them.

I looked around. Everybody was looking at me. I said, "Ya'll get out of here because I want to talk to Pierce in private. We'll be out in five minutes."

It was suggested later, by those I sent out of the dressing room, that I'd wanted that time alone with Pierce to beg for mercy. Or at least that was the general consensus outside.

That wasn't the truth. It was what I *should* have done, but I didn't. What I did do was tell Pierce that if he hit me any less than 100 percent I would not respect him and, furthermore, would never write a word about him. I said, "Listen, I used to be a burner and I think I still am. I ran a 9.6 hundred-yard dash and I think I can still go. And I got hands like Plaster of Paris and you can't make me drop that ball. You baby me and I'll know it and I'll simply walk off."

At that point he'd looked at me for a long second and I saw his eyes start to change. Nothing big, just enough to warn the wary. Except I wasn't smart enough to be wary. He said, "You sure you want it that way, Mr. Tippette?"

I said, "You damn right. Listen, do you know what speed can do? You're not ever going to get even a solid shot at me. I'll fake you out of your jock strap. Understood?"

His eyes changed a little more. I should have noticed. But he said, "Well, Giles, if you can run your feet as fast as you can run your mouth you ain't got anything to worry about."

Disrespect and no false modesty and he called me by my first name.

I should have shucked those pads right then and there and called it off. But there was one thing that was stopping me and it wasn't good sense. I knew I was suiting up for perhaps the last time in my life and, pain or no pain, I wanted that. It's the way old jocks think. It's why they have Old-Timers' games. It's why we get faster and tougher every year and tell more lies. It's the arena, and, pal, if you've never been there it can't be explained.

Pierce got up, standing now about eight-foot-seven and weighing in at a rough 500 pounds.

I went outside knowing I'd chosen the door with the tiger behind it, but I didn't give a damn.

And I hadn't had any iced tea either.

It was set up that I'd line up at a split end position and Pierce would line up at defensive end. Then I'd take a down-and-in, and the quarterback would fire me the ball, supposedly giving me time to put a move on Pierce. Unfortunately Jerry Vandergriff, who'd been a quarterback in his playing days, was the passer.

Now, so far as I know, I'd never done anything to hurt Jerry, consciously or otherwise. But there must have been something wrong with his arm that day because all he could do was loft the ball up in the air so that I was stretched out for the catch just as Pierce arrived. And whatever was wrong with his arm must have been hitting his funny bone because he kept giggling after every one of those collisions that weren't doing me any good. Finally I threw the ball at him and said, "Jerry, throw the damn thing! You are getting me killed!"

He finally did start zinging them in there but it didn't do any good. I tried every fake I knew on Pierce but he still found a way to be right in the way with those massive shoulders and arms all zeroed in on their target.

The ribs went about the seventh catch. After that it was grab the ball, turn, and take the lick in the small of my back. Pierce knew I was hurt, but all he said to me was, "This the way you want it?"

Through the teeth-clenched grin I said, "Yes."

It got over and we stuck around for a few more photographs and then I got in the car and told my wife, through those same clenched teeth, "Get me home."

Did it hurt? Not really that much. After the first lick Pierce put on me I was sort of anesthetized. You've read how, when a lion or tiger gets hold of its prey and gives it one good shake, the animal no longer feels any pain? That was how it was after that first collision with Pierce.

I remember lying on the ground, looking up at the sky, and wondering why it was getting dark so early. Then Randy Matthews came over and asked me if I was all right and I told him of course I was, that I'd be up shortly and wasn't about to miss a day of school over a little cold.

Or some such. I only have Randy's word for this and he just might lie if it suited him.

Anyway he popped an ammonia capsule under my nose and reality returned in large, unwelcome doses.

Pierce was still there.

Now I hadn't actually been too worried about getting hit. Even though some of the inner workings were wearing down I was still walking around on the skeleton of a fairly muscular body and I'd been hit plenty in the past. I'd been hit in football and baseball and rodeo and I just couldn't believe it could be that much different.

Except Randy's words, "the way the game is played today" kept coming back into my head.

There are a lot of expressions for hitters. He's a "hard hitter," he hits "a hunnert and ten percent," he'll "knock your socks off." I'd heard all those terms and been hit by some guys they'd applied to.

But Pierce called for brand-new expression. He was way beyond anything I'd ever heard about hitting. He was up there in the stratosphere. He was in another world. I'd expected a mortal and gotten a monster.

It's difficult to describe. I'd catch the ball and be going one way and then Pierce would arrive and we'd go the other way. It wasn't like running into a brick wall because brick walls don't engage you at some forty miles an hour. And I don't think it was like being hit by a freight train or a bus because I've never been hit by either. The closest, in my experience, was the time I'd had a head-on automobile collision with a pickup truck that had one of those stark grills obviously intended for knocking down gates, barn doors, and such. On that occasion I'd redesigned a steering wheel with my chest and proved to the insurance adjusters that, yes, a man could stick his head completely through a windshield.

But we did it one pass at a time. It wasn't all a haze. Sometimes I had moments of complete lucidity during which I could tell Randy what day it was and even what town we were in. I remember trying to explain to Pierce that when I'd told him I had hands of "Plaster of Paris" I'd meant *wet* Plaster of Paris. Not stone dry. The kind of plaster that just molds itself to the ball.

He'd just given me a strange look. I guess I hadn't been making all the sense I thought I was.

But his eyes never changed, not from the first hit to the last. I think if I'd said, "That's enough," they would have. But I'd challenged him on his turf. I'd insisted on no quarter, so I got none.

I spent a good three weeks healing and, during that time, I didn't enjoy sex, laughing, or a good sneeze. Pierce called in a few times to see how I was doing and I told him, of course, that I was doing fine. Why shouldn't I be? And what was he talking about? He said he'd heard that I'd been going down to the training room quite often and had just wondered why. He wondered if it had to do with our little fun game and if I might have gotten hurt a little bit.

He was back to being polite and humble and calling me "Mr. Tippette" again. Of course I told him that I hadn't been hurt, that I'd just gone to the training room to get Randy's help with a little bursitis in my shoulder.

And what did it all prove? That hitting a 50-year-old, over-the-hill jock made Pierce a pro football player? Of course not. Pierce was already a pro before he put on that 49er uniform. I just made the mistake of confusing a living-room manner with an on-the-field attitude. I'd figured a pro football player has got to be ready to traumatize his grandmother if she's got the ball. And Pierce was just so damn *nice* that I'd doubted his killer instincts.

Obviously my doubts have been erased.

And did going out there, nearly getting myself killed, prove that I could recapture youth? Of course not. But it did give me a glimpse back and that made the cracked ribs worth it.

It also answered another question. For years I'd been around and on the field with pro teams as a sportswriter, and the burning question had always come: "Hey, man, maybe you could have made it. Maybe you could have played."

That question no longer plagues me. There ain't enough

money in . . . name your place and it still wouldn't be enough money. I wouldn't take that kind of licking week after week for a standing date with the girl of your dreams.

So now I can sit back on the couch and watch Pierce on TV and see him being double teamed on the pass rush and say, "Hell, I went one-on-one with that guy. Big deal, doubling teaming. Now, if I was in there. . . ."

By the way, in case you were wondering, I didn't drop one of those 10 passes. But that's not the point. Come to think of it there isn't any point. All jocks, past and present, are crazy. Else they wouldn't do what they do. After you get hooked, reasons and points and sanity don't make much difference.

And you only understand if you have been there.

23

The Fifty-Three-Year-Old Anchor

About all that can be said about this particular particle of insanity is already in the story. The only thing I can add is about my wife. She'd heard all these big-time stories about my athletic past and she wanted to see some proof. I started off on a whim, but she turned it into a vendetta.

Thanks again to my three teammates on the sprint relay team who kept me from looking like a complete fool.

I decided I'd enter a track meet. Since I was just fifty-three years of age, it seemed like the ideal time to get back into active competition after only a thirty-year layoff.

Giving it some study, I thought I'd d up and enter the Hill Country Classic Masters meet in Mason, Texas, which draws entries from as far away as Hawaii and features some track and field people who hold the kinds of records you hope are misprints when you read about them in the paper.

I announced the decision to my wife.

That was a mistake. She gave me one of those looks that wives give husbands when they're of the opinion that the husband's brain has left town and said, "You'll just get hurt. You've disregarded all of the Surgeon General's warnings and the only exercise you've gotten is sneezing from all your allergies."

I had replied, somewhat loftily, "Listen, my girl, once an athlete, always an athlete. Don't sell me short."

Well, in a way she was right about the physical fitness program I'd enjoyed over all those years. I hadn't exactly been a couch potato, but, looking back, I figured out that the most physical exertion I'd undergone had been taking my youngest daughter to a rock concert in the early 1970s.

Still, I held to the credo that once an athlete always an athlete.

A fairly aloof attitude that I do not advise as the proper approach to a competition involving people who have been training since they got out of college.

But I went at it in the correct manner. I assessed my pluses and disregarded the minuses. As far as I was concerned, I was a unique combination of speed and strength. I'd thrown the shot in high school and in the Air Force, I'd run a 9.6 hundred-yard dash at Sam Houston State University, and I'd set an Interscholastic League Record for the 180-yard low hurdles in high school in 1952.

And I had five months to train. That was a world of time, even considering some of the Surgeon General's warnings. Not to mention my wife's.

I got hold of the times and distances for the last several years of the Hill Country track meet and thought, "Shoot! Look out here, boys. Somebody serious is coming to town."

I held that wonderful attitude right up to the time I got in competition with some of those folks. I guess I have to regard it as a learning experience.

But that was after. I figured what I'd do, seeing the times, was that I'd run the 110-meter high hurdles and put the shot. Go ahead and just get your basic third place in the shot and then blow them out in the hurdles.

So I said to myself, "Need upper body strength for the shot put." You have to understand that, as an athlete, I came along between the leather football helmet and the face mask. We didn't know anything about weight training and we thought a Nautilus was a submarine. Therefore it occured to me that I ought to hie myself off to a gym and learn something about getting strong the modern way.

I chose a place run by a fellow named Alan Anderson because it was called the Lone Star Gym, and, being a Texan, I thought that was a good sign. But mainly I chose it because after Alan had taken a hard look at me and I'd explained what I was after, he'd said, kind of tentatively, "Well, we can try."

What you want, when you've gotten yourself into the kind of situation I had, is an honest man.

I started training in the gym. Of course I was very new to the equipment; I'll tell about that later. What happened first was what my wife had originally predicted, but not exactly what she had in mind. A gym has all these mirrors around. They encircle the dang place. You can't move without a better look at your body than you want. And all these young guys are in there getting ready to go to Bermuda or Acapulco and stand on the beach and impress the girls. And you see yourself in the same mirror with these guys.

The dissimilarity between a fifty-three-year-old body and a twenty-year-old one is amazing.

It is also discomfiting and may even bother you. I promptly had an ulcer attack.

That cost five weeks of training and some loss in strength.

Now it gets better. Or worse, if you look at it from predictions made by my darker half. I kept working out in the gym because it was too cold to do any running outside. Within a week, working the weight equipment, I managed to spring both shoulders. They weren't all that sore. I could still brush my teeth, but my wife took great delight in shaking me awake at three o'clock in the morning to tell me I was moaning.

A bitter, know-it-all woman who, when I'd asked her to butter my toast, would just say, "Ha, ha, ha. You brought it on yourself, big boy."

Came spring and it was time to start working the legs, time to show the vaunted speed. Somebody asked if I was going to start off jogging. I just looked at him like his motor was out of place. I said, "Jogging is something you do to your memory when you want to remember something." I said, "Jogging is what non-jocks did in gym class in the sixth period. Jog? Hey, man, I run. Fast."

I began practicing starts. Went four, breezing it for about forty yards. Really felt good. Said to my wife, who was watching me, "I'm going to kick this one up at fifty yards."

Pulled a hamstring.

Friends, we are talking six weeks of recuperation. A dim glow started to enter my head that said, "Son, you cannot run the hurdles. This meet is less than two months away and you have not been over a flight of hurdles in yea these many years."

I said the hell with it. I could, too, run the hurdles.

So then I pulled one quadricep after the other.

I had, somehow, managed to make a friend of Randy Matthews,

the trainer at Angelo State University in my hometown of San
Angelo. One of the best in the business. I took my somewhat
shattered body over to Randy and had him take a look. His
personal opinion was that I'd better avoid the hurdles like a hay-
fever sufferer avoids ragweed.

So. Now we figure out the hundred meters and the shot put. To
the consortium of Alan Anderson, my strength coach, and Randy
Matthews, the trainer who's trying to hold me together, we have
now added Nat Sawyer, the coach at the local high school. He's
going to work with me on my starts.

Blew a calf muscle first time out of the blocks.

This, I know, is starting to sound like "General Hospital." What
was puzzling me was all these muscle pulls in my legs. I'm 6'3" and
weigh 210, but I've never been accused of having the kind of legs
that are considered examples of strength and form.

To tell the truth I've got skinny legs. Where, then, did all these
muscles I kept pulling come from? Randy Matthews said, "I don't
know, but I think you're slipping up on some kind of world record.
You are about to work me and three assistants to death. We didn't
treat this many injuries the entire last football season." Part of
some motivational confidence-building scheme, no doubt.

Nat Sawyer was *also* getting puzzled. We had decided that the
best thing I could do, as far as the sprint went, was to stay off my
legs. Nat had even suggested that maybe the best idea was not to
use them at all. Not even for walking.

But what was puzzling him was that my distance in the shot put
was going backwards.

That is the wrong direction. In a two-week period I'd managed
to drop four feet and it was four feet I couldn't afford to drop.

But while we were puzzling over that, Lee Graham, the director
of the meet, called and asked if I'd run a leg on the sprint relay.

By now, experience and Randy Matthews had made it clear that
there was no way I was going to sprint a hundred meters without
pulling something. He'd said, "I don't think I've ever seen it done
before, but you might dislocate a shoulder just running a sprint."

More confidence building.

It is one thing to run the open hundred and fall on your face.
It is quite another to let down three teammates in a sprint relay. So
I called Lee and told him my situation. He said it didn't matter,
said the guys I'd be running with didn't much care, that they

already had so many medals they were nearly out of room in their display cases.

The man was talking about help; the man was talking about dragging a cripple over the finish line.

I immediately said yes. Shows you what kind of character I've got.

But I was still slightly dispirited. Here I was going down to this masters meet, knowing I'd be up against some serious athletes, and all I was good at was hurting myself. I'd been fairly good in my time, but time passes, and my dauber was a little down. I wanted to be able to run with these guys, but I knew I couldn't. It was beginning to look as if Halloween might come a little early this year.

Came the meet. I walked up and finished dead last in the shot put. Reason I finished last was that a whole lot of guys threw it further than I did.

I was leaning over a fence afterwards, gasping for breath and trying to recuperate, when Lee Graham came running up and told me to come down and meet the other members of my sprint relay team. I have to tell you, frankly, that I didn't want to go. I didn't want to meet anyone, not even Candice Bergen, let alone guys who would be depending on me.

But I went down to the track to meet them. And enter Messers Wayne Bennet, Jim Cawley and Elias Mendiola. All of whom could run awful close to a 12 flat in the one hundred meters. Friends, in our age bracket, that is flying.

They were all so nice that a wave of guilt washed over me because I had a secret. I had somehow wandered around and entered myself in the hammer throw, an event I'd only seen in my nightmares before. I'd managed to get a bronze metal out of it, but I had also managed to pull a groin—muscle I didn't even know I had before it painfully let me know of its existence.

But there we were, setting up the team. I was trying to not walk with a limp. We decided that Elias with his explosive start would run the first leg, Cawley the second, Wayne Bennet the third, and I would try to anchor us in.

It was while Wayne and I were practicing hand-offs that he noticed something was the matter. He said, with a kind of puzzled frown, "Hell, you got to accelerate out. I'm going to hit that passing lane running full bore. You got to go or I'll run over you."

I whispered that I'd pulled a groin. He said, "Then you've got to withdraw."

I begged him not to tell the others. I told him I'd been training six months for this moment. I said, "I'll get it that last one hundred meters if I have to do it on my knees."

In my years of taking hand-offs in mile relays and sprint relays, the best hand-off I ever got was from Wayne Bennet. He came barreling in at top speed, knowing I couldn't accelerate, knowing I had a groin pulled, knowing he had to save me as much ground as he could in the 20-meters passing lane. I can still see him rounding that curve, gaining ground, stretching it out, that baton flashing in the sun, and placing it perfectly in my palm as I started to sprint.

We swept it. No, we didn't. Mendiola and Cawley and Bennet swept it. I was along for the ride. With the lead they gave me a woman carrying twins could have won.

But all that is not the point. The point is, I think, that there are some folks out there who don't know we're talking age limits. I saw a guy approaching sixty throw the shot about forty feet. Then I saw a seventy-eight-year-old try for the world's record in the four hundred meters. I saw some remarkable performances.

I once held the belief that once an athlete, always an athlete. That holds true if you pay the price in training and preparation. We would all like to go out there and repeat performances we gave in high school and college but it ain't gonna happen unless you lay your body on the line and get it to where it's gotta be.

I'm not embarrassed by how I did. The ones who ought to be embarrassed are the ones who finished behind me. Of course, they didn't have Bennet, Cawley, and Mendiola to help.

24

Roller Hockey Mayhem

The only difference between roller hockey and gang warfare in East Los Angeles is that they don't carry guns.

In roller hockey, I mean. Or, at least I didn't see any.

I was once mugged in New York City by four guys with drawn pistols. I believe I was less scared on that occasion that I was when I was out on the boards with the "guys."

If this story does, indeed, represent the end of my aging, almost-never-was, ex-jock athletic career, I have to figure I went out in a blaze of some kind.

I don't think it was glory.

I t took some doing and not a small amount of research, but I finally found a sport that I hadn't been physically damaged in.

I'm not talking about basketball or swimming or volleyball or any of those other girl's activities because I don't really consider them sports. I'm not being smug about this—it's just that I've always thought of sport as carrying some form of risk. Oh, of course I realize that swimmers get swimmer's ear and wrinkled fingers and toes and that volleyball players get skinned elbows. I've even observed that basketball players sprain their ankles and sometimes exchange harsh words with one another.

Well, so do pedestrians on busy streets.

No, I'm talking roller hockey here. And, believe me, it totally fulfills my risk criterion.

Most people have probably never heard of roller hockey, but it is a very viable sport. It has the unique distinction of being the only sport, besides honky-tonk brawls, that originated in West Texas. Supposedly it began back in 1953 in either Lubbock or Midland, but its origins are somewhat murky. No one seems to know why it got started in such an unlikely setting. I have a theory. I don't think it had anything to do with the game of ice hockey because, in those pre-TV-sports saturation days, I doubt there were more than nine people in all of West Texas who thought that ice hockey was anthing more than frozen cow dung.

No, my theory is that football season seemed a little short and, once it was over, all the players and ex-players and general rough-housers couldn't find a satisfactory outlet for their physical frustrations that wouldn't land them in jail. Until one night somebody lammed into somebody else at the roller rink and then a couple more got in the act and pretty soon there was roller hockey.

They say it became an organized sport sometime in the early 1960s. Well, if roller hockey abides by organized rules so do war and marriage and I don't consider either one of them team sports.

To be fair, it does have a governing body and leagues and all that good stuff and is scheduled to be a demonstration sport in the 1992 Olympics. They say the Russians are fervently trying to learn the game in time. I hope they do. I think they could learn a lot about international peace from getting on the boards with a few of those ol' West Texas boys. Might cause them to give unilateral disarmament even more thought.

We've got a cat and that cat has to be involved in everything that is going on. If my wife is sewing she's got to go over and help her. If I'm building a fire in the fireplace she's got to get right in the middle and supervise to make sure I lay the logs down just right. If we have company every guest has to be scrutinized and seen to pass inspection.

Well, I've always been that way about sports. Like the cat, here was something new that I had to stick my nose in. I'd tried just about everything else and here was something that definitely deserved investigation.

Except that I wasn't going to be able to do it from the outside. I'd have to be physically involved.

I also thought it would make a fitting climax to a life of relative insanity in relation to sports. I knew I was at the age where taking punishment was pretty well limited to reading without my glasses, but I thought I could get away with just one more thing.

Consequently I got hold of Milt Moody, who is the captain and center of the San Angelo team. The season was over, but he thought he could arrange an exhibition game with the Abilene team.

Sounded good to me.

Now roller hockey is very much like ice hockey except that they don't have ice and the puck is a hard rubber ball and they play on roller skates and somebody forgot about the penalty box. I could also see where it would have a great appeal for those good ol' boys from West Texas because not only do they get to knock the pudding out of each other but they also get to carry a stick so they can reach out and hit anything they might miss with their bodies.

Anyway, we got a game set up and I was going to participate. Toward that end, I'd invited some guests and I was going to do a story for a major magazine if everything worked out all right.

But then we discovered one rather limiting factor.

I couldn't skate. I don't mean I couldn't skate but just a little bit, I couldn't skate at *all.* The minute I got up on those eight wheels the faster I got a good look at the ceiling from the flat of my back. Monte Floyd, who owns the roller rink, worked with me long beyond the point of patience but it quickly became obvious that we were not talking about sex or bicycle riding. You *can* forget how to roller skate and I'd done it.

So there I was, a magazine piece to write, people coming to show off for.

And I couldn't skate.

Well, I panicked about it for a few days and then I went into a huddle with Milt Moody. We came up with a plan. I wouldn't actually enter the game as a participant but more as an irritant. What I'd do was heckle them from the sideline until Milt finally would tell me to get a stick and get out on the boards and see how well I could do.

The whole scam was based on one play. After I'd been challenged I'd come out on the boards and Milt would come skating down on the attack. I'd meet him at a mutually agreed upon spot because, remember, I couldn't skate. He'd appear to come into me full tilt, knocking me down and into a whirl as I hit the floor. As it happened he'd manipulate the ball so that it would end up in my hands and I'd turn, still lying on the floor, and hurl it into the net, thereby looking like a hero.

Toward this end the goalie, David Westbrook, who could probably have stopped a Sandy Koufax pitch, had been schooled to let anything I threw go in. He hadn't wanted to compromise his integrity to that degree, but a case of beer had convinced him.

There was just one thing wrong with this whole scenario. I'd told Milt, confidently, that I could handle the stunt, that I had once been a stuntman in the movies in Hollywood. He'd believed it because I'd told it with such conviction because I'd come to believe it.

But the plain fact was that I'd never been a stuntman. I'd been a stunt *double*. And that's about as big a difference as there is between the stand-in and the star. A stuntman is a guy you see leaping off 50-story buildings or being dragged by a horse or driving a car in a fiery crash. A stunt double, on the other hand, is someone who bears enough resemblance to the star to be photographed at long lens, and in my case I mean *looong* lens, riding the horse the star rides and wearing his clothes. I'd doubled for Rory Calhoun in some picture the name of which I have mercifully forgotten and for Gregory Peck in *MacKenna's Gold*. At no point was I ever asked to do more than gallop one of those tame remuda Hollywood horses across a flat plain.

But, through the years, I'd let my mouth run until I'd actually come to believe I'd been a stuntman and could do all those manipulations that real stuntmen do.

So I had Milt and myself convinced.

The day before, Milt and I practiced the gag at half speed. It had been my heartfelt conviction, and I'd told him so, that there was no point in leaving the game in the locker room, so let's just go through our paces in practice.

Worked beautifully. Milt would skate down on me, I'd try to high stick him, he'd fend me off, slam me with a shoulder, I'd whirl, drop, find the ball, and turn and heave it into the net.

Came out perfect everytime.

I'd also confided in him that this was to be my swan song from participation in physical athletics and I wanted to make it look good.

Milt was more than willing.

Of course I couldn't leave well enough alone. I figured we needed a little blood in the act so, for the edification and horror of my audience, I'd provide some. I went down to a novelty shop and bought some blood capsules, the fake kind that wrestlers and real stuntmen use; the kind you bite and that spill vegetable coloring down your chin and onto your front.

To check the effect, I practiced the night before when we had guests at the house. I came reeling out of the bathroom, one of the capsules tucked between my lower lip and my teeth, and then collapsed over the nearest wastebasket and bit the capsule. A satisfying stream of red came gushing out. One of the guests yelled, "My God, he's spitting up blood!"

My wife said, "I'll call a doctor!"

I looked around then, and said, "No, call a casting director."

Strangely enough, no one thought it was as funny as I did.

But my wife took it better than I thought she would, mainly, I think, because I was careful not to get a stain on the carpet.

But the next day came and the other dignitaries and I were lined up at rink-side to watch the play. Exhibition game or not, it was pretty excellent action. Once these roller hockey players get on deck they don't seem to care if it's practice or the world championship—they go all out. I got so involved in watching the scramble that it was a while before I remembered I had to go into my act. Finally, when Milt Moody came skating by our side of the rink, I yelled out, "What team are you, the Little Sisters of the Poor?"

He just looked at me.

A few minutes later I called out, "Is somebody hurt? Did I hear a whimper?"

By now the other members of both teams were looking over at me. None of them were in on the gag and the looks they were giving me were not what you'd call Christmas cards.

Then came a particularly vicious collision in the middle of the rink involving about five players. I yelled, "A dollar to the last one that bawls his little eyes out."

Boy, now I was getting some looks. It came to a head when Milt came skating by and I said, "Look at that! Forty years old and still hasn't lost his skate key."

That did it. Milt called time and came up to the wall and said to me, "Get a stick."

I said, "Whaaat?"

Milt said, "Get a stick and get out here."

I was acting, but if he was, Brando could have taken lessons.

I felt my invited guests drawing away from me.

But I was still full of bluster. I said, "Hell, yes. I'll come out there and I want to see you get by me one time. Just one time."

He said, "Get a stick."

Somebody handed me a stick and I was helped out onto the rink, taking a position about ten feet and slightly to the right of the net. They had a face-off at midrink and lo and behold Milt ended up with the ball and came skating toward me.

Now, a word about roller-hockey skaters. They bear about as much resemblance to a kid on the sidewalk as Wayne Gretzky does to those people skating at Rockefeller Plaza. They can skate backwards, forwards, and sideways, sometimes all three at once. They can knock you down, take the ball away from you and be gone without losing a stride.

And I was on the same floor with these people.

Then here came ol' Milt bearing down on me. Never mind about our little plot, never mind about our friendly talks, never mind about any of that. I'd challenged the man and that was the last thing he remembered.

Milt is built like a middle linebacker for the Chicago Bears. I didn't have time to get a radar gun on him, but I figured he was skating at me at about 140 miles an hour.

He came on and I moved a half step to my right to meet him, raising my stick as I did. I had the blood capsule comfortably tucked under my lip and was working it up between my teeth to where I could bite through it at the appropriate second. I remember thinking, "This is going to work fine. Just fine."

After all, we'd rehearsed it and, beyond that, I'd been a Hollywood stuntman.

Except that, in the last split instant, Milt was coming much too fast and I suddenly remembered I hadn't been a stuntman at all. I was late getting up with my stick and Milt caught me square in the chest with his shoulder. Our rehearsal had called for me to cushion his blow with my hands and then to whirl and fall. I whirled and fell all right, but it wasn't the graceful move we'd practiced. It was more like a wham, ouch, clunk.

But, true to the script, Milt delivered the ball into my hands which I was supposed to struggle up and throw into the net behind me.

Now I had bitten the blood capsule, though not consciously. Actually, I needn't have, because things began to go a bit awry at that point. Milt and I had overlooked a fine point. The net I was supposed to throw the ball into was the net that David Westbrook was guarding. And that was the same net I was supposed to be guarding.

There are five players on a roller hockey team, including goalies, and all of them, my own erstwhile teammates included, swarmed on me as I was struggling to get to my knees to throw the ball past David. My so-called teammates were confused because I was pulling a Wrong Way Corrigan and they were trying to stop me because they weren't in on the joke. The other team just wanted to knock the hell out of me and get the ball. For about five seconds I was the object of attention of more hockey sticks than I ever again want to see. I finally got hold of the ball and made a kind of fadeaway shot backwards that David, true to bribery, managed to gather up and sweep into the net.

I was wearing a white shirt, deliberately, and the front was soaked red. Milt, looking really concerned, helped me off the rink asking if I was all right. I just shook my head, not answering. I had a real good reason for that.

Heading out, I just nodded my head at my wife, telling her I was going home and she should take care of what company remained.

Neither Milt, nor anyone else besides my wife, had known about the blood capsule. That was just as well. I was glad to see that concern in Milt's eyes. He ought to have been concerned. He'd damn near killed me.

I went home and washed my mouth out, removing all the fake blood from the capsule. But when my wife came home with a guest I was sitting on the couch mopping the real blood off my knees and elbows and spitting real blood into the wastebasket I'd been so cute with the night before.

So much for my delusions that I'd been a stuntman.

During my less-than-average career as an athlete it had some-times been suggested that I talked a better game than I played. If that were true I had come to a fitting end because, in that collision with Milt, I had managed to bite the end of my tongue off. Which effectively shut my mouth for a time.

And I hadn't even needed that blood capsule. It had just been money wasted.

Why in the hell hadn't Milt and I figured on that from the start? Dammit, you never think of these things until it's too late.

I was secretly glad that I'd gone out for the last time with a real bang instead of just talk about a bang.

But you know what? I've changed my mind. I have not yet accepted that there is a last time. Not so long as there's still some game, somewhere.